EAST SUSSEX SHIPWRECKS
OF
THE 19TH CENTURY

(PEVENSEY – HASTINGS – RYE)

EAST SUSSEX SHIPWRECKS OF THE 19TH CENTURY
(PEVENSEY – HASTINGS – RYE)

David Renno

The Book Guild Ltd
Sussex, England

First published in Great Britain in 2002 by
The Book Guild Ltd
25 High Street
Lewes, East Sussex
BN7 2LU

Copyright © David Renno 2002

The right of David Renno to be identified as the author of this work has been asserted by him in accordance with the Copyright, Designs and Patents Act 1988.

All rights reserved. No part of this publication may be reproduced, transmitted, or stored in a retrieval system, in any form or by any means, without permission in writing from the publisher, nor be otherwise circulated in any form of binding or cover other than that in which it is published and without a similar condition being imposed on the subsequent purchaser.

Typesetting in Times by
Acorn Bookwork, Salisbury, Wiltshire

Printed in Great Britain by
Antony Rowe Ltd, Chippenham, Wiltshire

A catalogue record for this book is available from
The British Library.

ISBN 1 85776 647 4

CONTENTS

Foreword	vii
Introduction	ix
Types of Sail Rigging	1
Vessel Sail Rigging	2
Storm Warnings	4
Beaufort Wind Scale	6
South Coast Martello Towers	7
Coastguards	11
Shipwreck Recovery	13
Mariners 'Dispatch Box' Invention	14
Details of Shipwrecks	21
Sources of Information	281
Acknowledgements	283
Alphabetical Index of Shipwrecks	284

FOREWORD

David Renno has brought together a feast of local, regional and international maritime history by reconstructing the stories of many ships that mostly fell foul of the weather and were either sunk in the English Channel or were cast ashore on the East Sussex coast.

Most were wooden sailing vessels of many types, but as the century progressed we find the introduction of iron steamers. Cargoes ranged from bullion to ballast, though most were of mundane materials such as coal, chalk, sand, grain, iron and timber, showing that the ships were the maritime version of today's lorries carrying bulk cargoes. Most were from England, with many from France, but others were Dutch, German, Swedish, Prussian, Belgian, Canadian, Danish, Norwegian, Russian and Italian, underlining the multicultural nature of seafaring tradition then, as now.

The story of each ship in distress is an intimate window on our late Georgian and Victorian past, telling us much about the men, the trade patterns, and the rescue services – particularly the lifeboats and the coastguards. But most of all they tell us of the great heroism of people battling against unexpected situations, and in spite of terrible adversity many lives were saved.

Although the loss of life and property then had tragic effects on families for many years, the partial survival of some wrecks now as archaeological sites gives us a further opportunity to study the past in intimate detail. The protection and careful investigation of those historic wrecks is therefore of considerable importance to future generations, for it is all too easy to destroy them by casual salvage and treasure hunting. This book will therefore give future generations of researchers an important opportunity of understanding the stories of these 'East Sussex Shipwrecks of the 19th Century'.

Peter Marsden
Shipwreck Heritage Centre, Hastings.

INTRODUCTION

The stories of the vessels mentioned in this book have, in the main, been researched from local news reports. However, it will be appreciated that such news reports were not generally available much before the middle of the 19th century. A consequence of this is that the details of the earlier recorded shipwrecks are less full, and in some cases are almost non-existent, but these are included with whatever details are available. Similarly, not all the information is known about each feature of every vessel. However, what information is known is detailed for each shipwreck.

The very nature of reporting mishaps at sea during most of this period was only made possible when either the members of the crew were saved or when a vessel failed to arrive at its destination, bearing in mind that travelling by sea between continents then took considerably longer than it does today. The reporting of sea disasters was therefore often not made until days or weeks after the event, unless there were other vessels involved in any rescue attempt. In these cases the rescue was invariably within coastal waters, such as those recorded within this book between the towns of Pevensey and Rye in East Sussex.

Along the East Sussex coast between Pevensey and Rye there was only one harbour, that being at Rye. If vessels therefore wished to discharge or load a cargo elsewhere, then the vessel generally had to be beached for the purpose. However, in bad weather and sea conditions, beached vessels were very vulnerable unless it was possible to haul them up the beach beyond the sea. This was often not possible, especially when a vessel was fully laden. It was therefore generally safer for the vessel to ride the bad weather out at sea than sat on the beach at the mercy of the weather. It was hence an unfortunate fact of life that vessels that were beached to discharge their cargo were uninsurable.

The shipwrecks in this book are shown in chronological order of loss. Those seeking information on a particular named vessel should refer to the Alphabetical Index at the back of the book.

TYPES OF SAIL RIGGING

Fore-and-aft Where the vessel's sails are set parallel, or close to, the fore and aft center-line of the vessel.

gaf A type of fore-and-aft rigging where the largest sail on a mast is four-sided, with its leading edge attached to the mast.

lug Also a type of fore-and-aft rigging where the largest sail on a mast is again four-sided, with either the fore edge projecting forward of the mast, or the uppermost part of the sail projecting forward of the mast.

sprit A type of fore-and-aft rigging where a four-sided sail is held in place on a long spar or sprit.

square The sails are attached to spars which are at right angles to the mast, and on the fore-and-aft centre-line of the vessel.

VESSEL SAIL RIGGING

barge Flat-bottomed freight vessel with or without sails.

barque/barquentine At least a three-masted vessel with aftermost mast fore-and-aft rigged with the other masts square-rigged.

brig/brigantine Two-masted vessel with one fore mast square-rigged and the other mast fore-and-aft rigged.

chasse-maree French 2–3 masted vessel, lug rigged.

cutter Single-masted vessel rigged like a sloop but with a running bowsprit.

galliot Two-masted vessel for North Sea and coastal work, with one gaff-rigged sail on the main mast and the mizzen mast with up to three square sails.

ketch Two-masted vessel fore-and-aft rigged, with the mizzen mast stepped forward of the rudder.

lugger Lug-rigged vessel.

schooner Two- or more masted vessel with fore-and-aft rigging, where the masts are of either equal height, or where the foremost mast is lower than the after-mast.

sloop Single-masted vessel fore-and-aft rigged with mainsail and jib.

smack Single-masted gaff-rigged fishing or coastal vessel.

snow Two-masted vessel square-rigged like the brig.

STORM WARNINGS

In 1861 a system was devised to indicate to mariners the impending bad weather conditions for that area. As far as Hastings was concerned the Mayor, T. Ross Esq., published in November 1861 directions as to the use of this system which consisted of the following signs.

- *'The drum'*: a black square. This indicated that storm-force winds may be expected from nearly opposite quarters successively.
- *'The cone'*: a triangle. When the point of the triangle was pointing upwards, a storm was due first from the north. If the point of the triangle was pointing downwards, then a storm was due first from the south.
- *'The cone and drum'*: indicated that dangerous winds were expected first from the direction as indicated by the point of the cone.

These signs were displayed until dusk of that day, upon receipt of a telegram from London indicating impending bad weather. It was stressed however, that these bad weather warnings were of a general nature and that mariners should use their own experience, judgement and local barometer readings. At Hastings it was suggested that these barometer readings, from the local meteorological society, should be displayed in a conspicuous position for the benefit of all mariners using the Hastings beach.

The use of the 'drum' and 'cone' system in conjunction with barometer readings was emphasised by Admiral Fitzroy who said:

> 'Speaking generally, there is far less occasion to give warning of southerly storms by signal than of northerly, because those from the southward are preceded by notable signs in the atmosphere, by falling barometer, and by a temperature higher than usual at the season; whereas, on

the contrary, dangerous storms from a polar quarter (north west to north east) are sometimes sudden, and are usually preceded by a rising barometer, which often misleads uninformed persons, especially if accompanied by a temporary lull, of perhaps a day or two, with an appearance of fine weather.'

BEAUFORT WIND SCALE

Force	Wind Speed (Knots)	Wind Description
1	1 – 3	Light
2	4 – 6	Light
3	7 – 10	Light
4	11 – 16	Moderate
5	17 – 21	Fresh
6	22 – 27	Strong
7	28 – 33	Strong
8	34 – 40	Gale
9	41 – 47	Severe gale
10	48 – 55	Storm
11	56 – 63	Violent storm
12	64 +	Hurricane force

SOUTH COAST MARTELLO TOWERS

The inclusion of these towers is as a reference aid, because some of the shipwrecks were at or nearby such towers. The known location of each tower between Pevensey and Rye is shown below, and, where known, its fate. However, no trace survives of most of them. Having mentioned the Martello Towers it would seem remiss if a very short history of these towers was not given.

By the year 1804, Napoleon Bonaparte had gathered together a vast army on the French coast near Calais, with the quite obvious intention of invading England. However, as can be appreciated, to convey such a large army across the English Channel without suffering great losses was a very difficult problem for him, especially as the English Navy at this time were in total control of the Channel.

On the English side of the Channel there were the inevitable discussions and meetings as to how best defend the country against this threat, if it eventually turned into a reality. One participant in these discussion was a Captain William Ford, who suggested the idea of Martello Towers. It is assumed, and is probably correct, that his idea was developed from his knowledge of the tower at Mortella Point, in the Bay of Fioprenzo, on the island of Corsica. Hence the name 'Martello' would appear to have been a derivative from the location of this tower at Mortella Point.

William Pitt, who was the Prime Minister of the day, agreed that a number of these towers should be built between Folkestone in Kent and Beachy Head, near Eastbourne, in East Sussex. To enhance the country's defence against an impending French invasion, Pitt also authorised the building of a 30 foot (9m) wide canal (the Royal Military Canal) between Shorncliffe (Kent) to Pett Level (East Sussex), at a cost of £200,000. It is clearly obvious to the present-day observer (and also it must be said to some people at the time) that a 30ft-wide canal would probably have little or no effect whatsoever on the French army, when it is considered that to have reached this canal they had just crossed the English Channel.

It is just as well that neither the Martello Towers nor the Royal Military Canal were called upon to defend the country, as the French army never invaded, being defeated at Waterloo by the Duke of Wellington in 1815.

The prime minister having agreed to the building of the Martello Towers, by 1808 73 had been built at a cost of £3,000 each, approximately 600 yards (548m) apart, along the south coast between Folkestone and Beachy Head. The towers were numbered 1 to 73 from east to west, with two redoubt forts to act as a base for supplies, and for overall control, at Dymchurch in Kent and at Eastbourne in East Sussex. A further 29 towers were built along the east coast by 1812, between Brightlingsea in Essex and Aldeburgh in Norfolk, being identified by letters starting 'A' at Brightlingsea and ending with 'CC' in Aldeburgh.

Each 30ft-high brick built tower was constructed in an inverted flower pot design using half a million bricks. The walls were smooth and tapered so as to deflect enemy cannon fire and to allow a wider downward firing range of the gun mounted on the roof of each tower. The towers were constructed such that the sea-facing part of the tower was approximately 13 feet (4m) thick, whereas the land-facing part was only about 6 feet (2m) thick.

Each tower had three levels. The ground floor was used for the storage of munitions and provisions, and access was by ladder from the first floor. To prevent accidental explosions of the stored munitions, the lanterns used for light were separated from the munitions by glass. The entrance to the tower was on the first floor and access was gained to the tower entrance by either ladder or drawbridge from the ground. The flooring above the munitions store was secured by wooden pegs instead of metal nails so as to prevent any risk of explosion or fire. The first floor was divided into three parts in order to house one officer and the 24 men of the Royal Artillery, who manned these towers. The upper floor of the tower, or the roof area, was the tower's gun platform. Access to it from the floor below was by means of a staircase built into the outer wall of the tower. However, the door from these stairs to the gun platform always had to be kept closed when the cannon was being used, to prevent flashback. This required the door to have a hole in it so that ammunition could be passed through, but this hole itself had to have a cover over it. The cannon mounted on the roof, which was capable of being turned in any direction to be fired, was a two and a half ton gun capable of firing a 24 pound (11kg) shot over a mile (1.6km). It will be appreciated, therefore, that as these towers were on average only 600yds (548m) apart, any enemy vessel approaching the shore could be reached by the cannons of over a dozen different Martello Towers.

What is known of the fate of the towers is shown below.

Martello Towers

Tower	Note on location	Fate
28	On the estuary west bank of the river Rother at Rye Harbour. Known as the Enchantress Tower. Close to Frenchman's Beach caravan park.	
29	At the mouth of Rye Harbour.	Destroyed by the sea soon after construction.
30	West of Rye on the Winchelsea Road, now over 2 miles (3km) inland. The most inland of any Martello Tower, it was sited in order to protect the Royal Military Canal, and the River Brede and River Rother sluices.	
31–38	Equally spaced over a 2 mile (3km) stretch in front of Pett Level on the shingle beach. Starting with Tower no. 31 at Dogs Hill and ending with Tower no. 38 at Cliff End, which is at the western end of the Military Canal.	Tower nos. 35 and 38 destroyed by the Army, April 1872. Tower no. 37 also destroyed by the Army, June 1864.
39	Tower nos. 39–43 were equally spaced between Bo-Peep in west St Leonards and Bulverhythe on the Bexhill/St Leonards border.	
40	See Tower no. 39.	

Tower	Note on location	Fate
41	See Tower no. 39.	
42	See Tower no. 39.	Demolished in 1842. Bricks used to build St Marks Church, Little Common, Bexhill.
43	See Tower no. 39.	
44	Towers 44–54 were spaced between Galley Hill, Bexhill and Rock House Bank, west of Pevensey sluice.	
45	See Tower no. 44.	
46	See Tower no. 44.	
47	See Tower no. 44.	
48	See Tower no. 44.	Demolished. Bricks used to build extension to St Marks Church, Little Common, Bexhill in 1845.
49	See Tower no. 44.	
50	See Tower no. 44.	
51	See Tower no. 44.	
52	See Tower no. 44.	
53	See Tower no. 44.	
54	See Tower no. 44.	Destroyed in 1900.
55	This was one of the towers fitted with a semaphore machine. Now a residence.	

The approximate position of each of the Martello Towers between Rye Harbour and Pevensey are shown on Plate 5 on page 18.

COASTGUARDS

In 1892 there were a total of 15 coastguard stations along the coastline between Jury's Gap and Pevensey. Those involved in rescues from the vessels in the following pages are shown on *Plate 6* on page 19. However, below is a list of all these coastguard stations, together with details of their rescue equipment and the recorded mileage between each of them.

Coastguard stations, c. 1892

Name of station	Rescue equipment	Distance from preceding station (miles/kilometres)
Jury's Gap	Rocket apparatus	5 (8)
Camber	Lifeboat	2 (3)
Rye Harbour	Belts and lines	1 (1.6)
Winchelsea	Lifeboat	1 (1.6)
Dog's Hill	Belts and lines	2 (3)
Pett	Rocket apparatus	3 (5)
Haddocks	Belts and lines	1 (1.6)
Fairlight	Belts and lines	2 (3)
Ecclesbourne	Belts	3 (5)
Marine Parade	Lifeboat	
	Belts and lines	2 (3)
Priory	Belts and lines	1 (1.6)
Bo Peep	Rocket apparatus	2 (3)
Bexhill	Belts and lines	3 (5)
Kewhurst	Belts and lines	2 (3)
Pevensey	Rocket apparatus	2 (3)

On 25th April 1859 the first test of the rocket apparatus supplied in the Hastings area was carried out off Marine Parade, Hastings. The test was supervised by the district coastguard commander, Captain

Gough, RN in company of his clerk, Mr Bulley. The object of the apparatus was to enable the coastguard to get a line to a stricken ship and then be able to use the line to rescue the crew.

At about 1pm that afternoon, two coastguard galleys were moored approximately 400 yards (365m) offshore, and parallel to it, with a rope between each. The object of the test was to fire the rocket apparatus so that the line went over the rope stretched between the two galleys. The first two attempts were successful, but the third went to the east of both boats. This appeared to be due to one of the legs of the rocket launcher having sunk into the beach from the effect of the previous two firings.

A simulated test was also carried out of hauling persons ashore using this apparatus. This simulation required one end of a strong rope to be securely anchored in the beach while the other end was fixed to the top of the West Hill. A volunteer coastguardsman then got into the 'Breeches Buoy', consisting of a lifebuoy and canvass strop, and was then hauled along the rope by a line working a block from the beach end of the rope, up to the West Hill. This first test was totally successful, as was the second.

SHIPWRECK RECOVERY

In 1859 it was becoming of great concern to the Board of Trade that the value of shipping and the cargoes that were being lost at sea had reached £2,750,000. It was not only the value of the loss that was of concern but that a large proportion of the cargoes might well be salvaged if prompt and efficient action was taken. Thus far, there had been a great reluctance on behalf of owners and insurers alike to make any attempts to recover vessels and/or their cargoes. It was estimated at this time that about 150,000 tons of shipping were lost annually.

In an attempt to resolve this problem, the Patent Derrick Company was established at 27 Cornhill, London. This company had a number of floating derricks stationed at various points around the coast, which were designed to salvage shipwrecked vessels and their cargoes from the seabed.

A similar company existed in America and had been extremely successful in recovering shipwrecks. This company, the New York Derrick Company, had salvaged several hundred vessels and was so successful that it was paying a yearly dividend to its shareholders of 40 per cent.

MARINERS 'DISPATCH BOX' INVENTION

As mentioned in the Preface, the circumstances or details of a ship's demise was often not known to the outside world for some considerable time after the event, especially for those vessels sailing across oceans and between continents. It was this, and her deep interest in the well-being of sailors generally, that caused a Mrs Dean, who lived in the Clive Vale area of Hastings, to turn her mind to this invention in 1881.

Mrs Dean's idea was based on the principle of a lifeboat. It was a small unsinkable vessel that would not capsize and was to be carried on ships that went to sea. The idea was that when a ship was facing disaster the crew should write down the details of the ship and their circumstances and anything else they deemed of some importance, and put this information inside the 'dispatch box' on the deck of the small unsinkable vessel and throw it into the sea – the theory being that at some stage the wind and tides would eventually bring the small vessel to shore with its information on board, so that the world at large could then be made aware of the ship's fate.

Mrs Dean's design was of a small yacht about 3 feet 6 inches (1.15m) long, painted light blue, with the words 'Jesus Christ came into this world to save sinners' painted on the sails in phosphorous, so as to be legible both night and day. Mrs Dean took her idea to Mr F. Tutt, a local man, who built the vessel for her. Once completed it was handed over to Mr Smith, the chief officer of Hastings coastguard, for him to find a suitable ship to test the invention. He eventually found that Captain Breach, the master of a ship called the *Jerusalem*, was more than interested in the idea and readily agreed to take the invention on his next voyage to test it. However, before that, the 'dispatch box' was tested in the sea off Hastings and it was found to travel at 4 to 5 miles (6–8km) an hour in a moderate wind.

With the trial a success, the 'dispatch box' was sent to Captain

Breach at Gravesend in Kent, from where he set sail on 11th March 1881, passing off Hastings at 3pm the following day. It was his plan to launch the 'dispatch box' when 300 miles (482km) from the Scilly Isles. The 'dispatch box' contained six stamped addressed envelopes to Mrs Dean, six to Mr Smith of Hastings coastguard, and six to Captain Breach at Melbourne. There was also a request to the finder of the 'dispatch box' to write to the above persons giving details of how and where it was found and if it was at sea to relaunch it with the request for any subsequent finder to do likewise. Captain Breach said that on the day he first launched the 'dispatch box' from the *Jerusalem* he would give the crew half a day's holiday and an extra glass of grog each and would name the 'dispatch box' *Little Jerusalem*.

It was anticipated that *Little Jerusalem* would be found by one of the many homeward-bound vessels that passed by the Scilly Isles. However, that was not to be the case because nearly three months later, on 6th June 1881, *Little Jerusalem* was discovered on the shore in County Galway, Ireland, by a local fisherman. He took the little vessel to a Mr Collier of the coastguard station at Arran and in accordance with the instructions relaunched it and wrote to Mrs Dean and Mr Smith of finding it in Ireland. In his letters to them he said that *Little Jerusalem* was slightly damaged at the keel, which was probably due to hitting the rocks where it was found.

There is no indication that this idea was ever used again beyond this trial. However, if nothing else, it proved the idea could work, even though it could take months for news to reach the outside world, although at least it would be known what happened and where. [Ref. HN 12.3.1881; HC 15.6.1881]

Plate 1. **Nerissa.** Ashore at Hastings 11th November 1891. By kind permission of Hastings Library

Plate 2. **J.C. Pfluger.** Ashore at Hastings 11th November 1891. By kind permission of Hastings Library

Plate 3. **Marine Parade Coastguard Station, Hastings.** By kind permission of Hastings Library

Plate 4. **Lamburn.** Ashore at Hastings 18th November 1866. Copyright Michael Myers

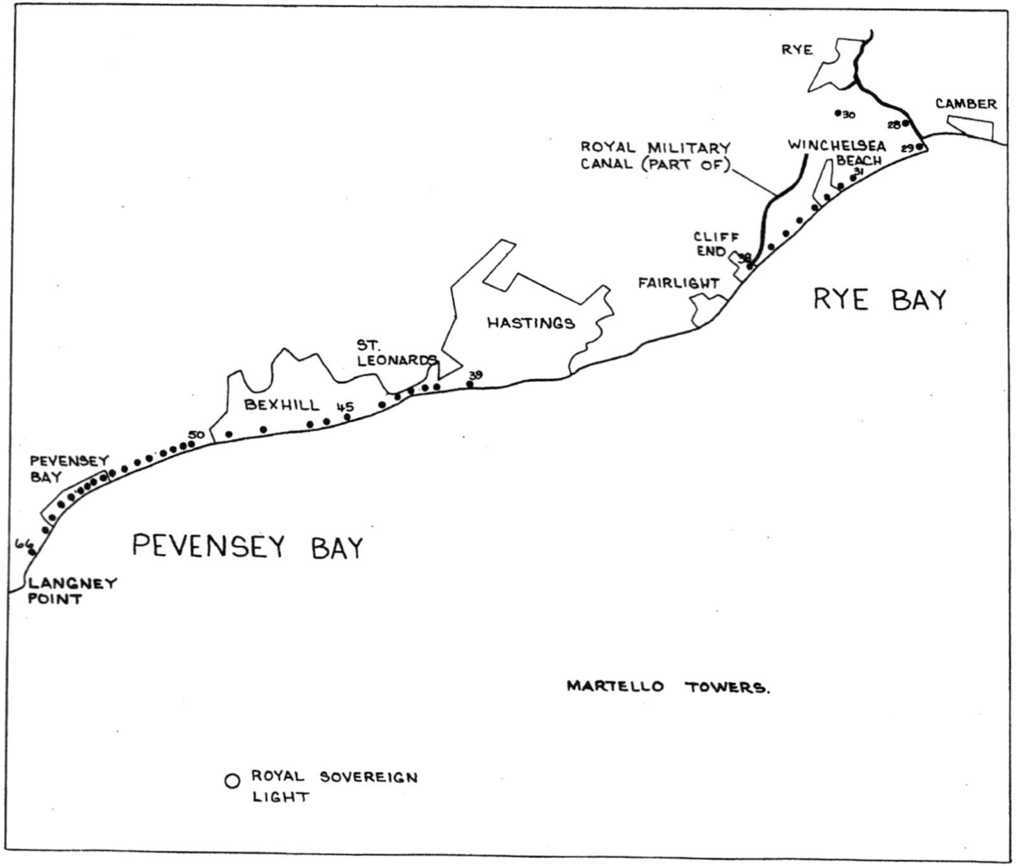
RYE
CAMBER
30
28
29
ROYAL MILITARY
CANAL (PART OF)
WINCHELSEA
BEACH
31
CLIFF
END
38
FAIRLIGHT
RYE BAY
HASTINGS
ST.
LEONARDS
39
BEXHILL
45
50
PEVENSEY
BAY
66
PEVENSEY BAY
LANGNEY
POINT
MARTELLO TOWERS.
ROYAL SOVEREIGN
LIGHT

Plate 5

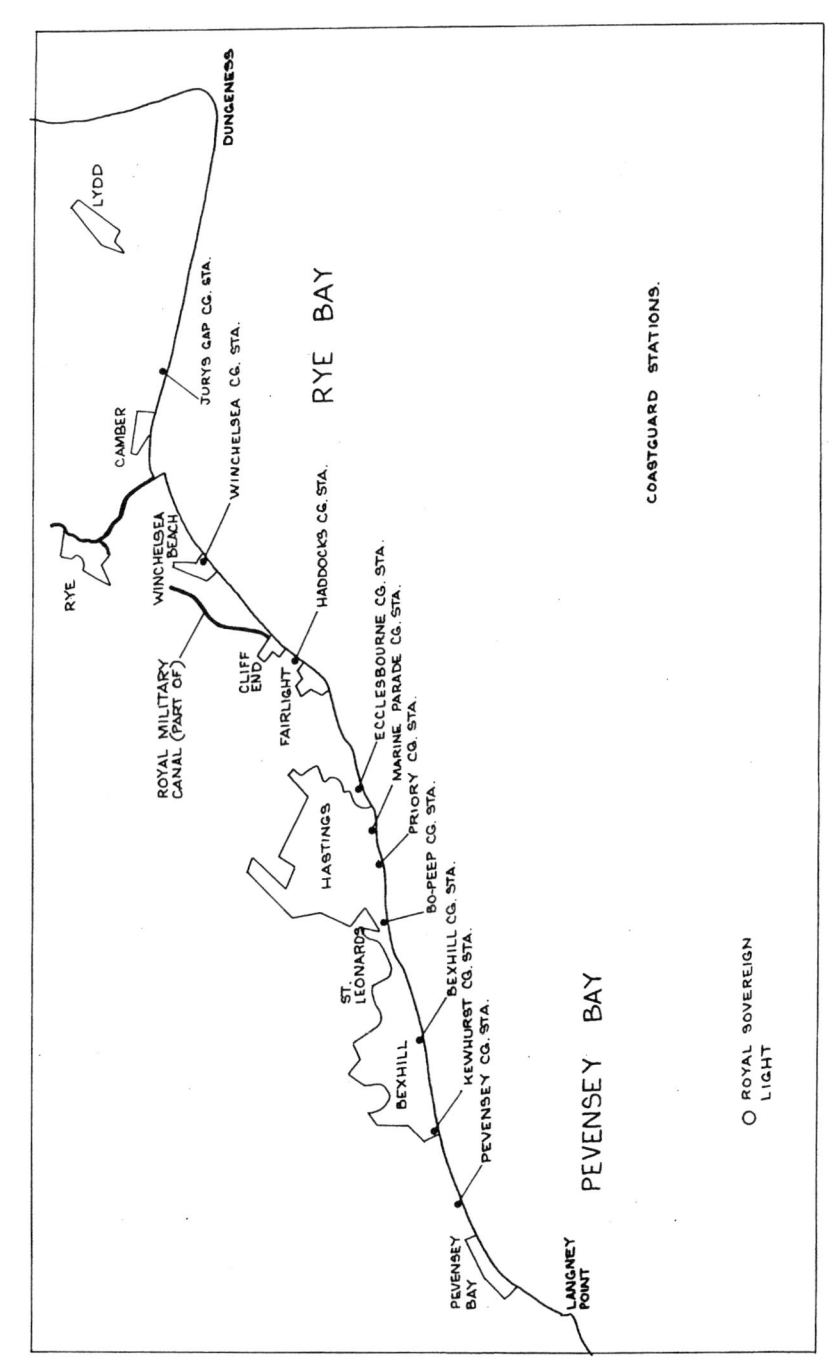

Plate 6

Plate 7. **Linnet/Henrietta.** 9th March 1891. Sketches of the damage and the men who lost their lives. By kind permission of the Hastings & St Leonards Observer

DETAILS OF SHIPWRECKS

KEY TO REFERENCE SOURCES

BC	Bexhill Chronicle
BPCP	Brett Premier Cinque Ports
BHB	Brett Historical Biographies
BMSS	Brett Manuscripts
CPC	Cinque Ports Chronicle
EC	Eastbourne Chronicle
EG	Eastbourne Gazette
FC	Folkestone Chronicle
FE	Folkestone Express
FO	Folkestone Observer
HA	Hastings & St Leonards Advertiser
HC	Hastings & St Leonards Chronicle
HG	Hastings & St Leonards Gazette
HI	Hastings & St Leonards Independent
HN	Hastings & St Leonards News
HO	Hastings & St Leonards Observer
HS	Hastings & St Leonards Standard
HT	Hastings & St Leonards Times
JRD	John Reeley Diary
LL	Lloyds List
LR	Lloyds Register
MCA	Maritime & Coastguard Agency Records
RS	Remarkable Shipwrecks
RNLI	Royal National Lifeboats Institute Records
SIBI	Shipwrecks Index of British Isles
SEA	South Eastern Advertiser
SES	South Eastern Sail
SE	Sussex Express
SWA	Sussex Weekly Advertiser

Innocenza Protetta

Date sunk: 14.11.1800
Location: Rye Bay
Type: Spanish
Voyage: London to Lisbon
Ref: SIBI V2 section 3

Adriana

Date sunk:	30.11.1802
Location:	Hastings
Type:	Dutch Brig
Cargo:	Lemons, raisins, wine and general goods
Voyage:	Malaga to Rotterdam
Master:	Dehler
No. of crew:	7
Ref:	SIBI V2 section 3; BPCP V4 p102; SWA 6.12.1802

This vessel was driven ashore in a violent storm with the loss of the mate and three crew. However, the master and three further crew were saved.

As a matter of interest, a week later and unrelated to this wreck, there was an auction held at the Custom House, Hastings on 8th December 1802 at 11am. The advertisement for the auction read as follows:

For sale, on Wednesday the 8th day of December, 1802, at eleven o'clock in the forenoon, IN SUNDRY LOTS, THE FOLLOWING GOODS

About 1744 gallons Geneva [a type of gin]
480 gallons Brown Brandy For private use
90 gallons White Brandy
170 gallons Rum, legal strength for dealers

The goods may be viewed the day before and morning of the sale. Twenty five per cent deposit will be required.

Attempt

Date sunk:	13.12.1803
Location:	Off Rye
Voyage:	London to Rye
Master:	Plasskett
Ref:	SIBI V2 section 3

Nelly

Date sunk:	2.11.1810
Location:	Between Hastings and Bexhill
Type:	British sailing vessel
Home port:	Sunderland
Ref:	SIBI V2 section 3

This vessel was being pursued by a French privateer and in its attempt to escape it hit rocks near Bexhill and became a loss.

Hopewell

Date sunk:	11.12.1810
Location:	Rye Bay
Type:	British sloop
Cargo:	Wheat
Home port:	Barmouth
Master:	Roberts
Ref:	SIBI V2 section 3; BHB V2 p110

This sloop was out in Rye Bay in a severe gale and heavy seas when she was driven ashore somewhere between Hastings and Rye, with the loss of all hands.

Commerce

Date sunk:	11.12.1810
Location:	Rye Bay
Type:	British brig
Ref:	BHB V2 p110

This vessel, like the *Hopewell* (see page 27), was out in Rye Bay when it was driven ashore in a severe gale between Hastings and Rye, with the loss of all hands and the £10,000 cargo.

Brothers

Date sunk:	13.1.1811
Location:	Ashore at Bexhill
Type:	British brig
Cargo:	General provisions
Home port:	Weymouth
Voyage:	*En route* from Ross to unknown destination
Master:	Robert Jameson
Ref:	SIBI V2 section 3; SWA 21.1.1811; BPCP V4 p200

At about 11pm on Sunday 13th January 1811, the *Brothers*, under the command of the Master, Robert Jameson from Ross in Ireland, was driven ashore at Bexhill by a French privateer intent on capturing the vessel. At the time a severe south-west storm was blowing with mountainous seas which made escape from the French vessel almost impossible. The privateer was after the *Brothers'* cargo of mutton, beef, lard and other general goods, worth £10,000.

Once the vessel was ashore all the crew managed to get onto the beach safely and were looked after by the Hastings custom authorities and a contingent of the 11th Royal Victoria Battalion stationed at Bexhill barracks, under the command of Lieutenant Kennedy. Kennedy's men also manned a guard over the vessel and its cargo until the cargo could be taken off the following day. Once taken off the *Brothers*, the cargo was stored in warehouses belonging to Messrs S. and A. Brooks who acted as agents for the owner of the cargo, together with James Breeds and James Russell.

Unknown stone sloop

Date sunk:	11.10.1813
Location:	Ashore at Bexhill
Cargo:	Stone
Home port:	Hastings
Owner:	Messrs Breeds, Hastings
Ref:	BPCP V1 p59

This vessel was off Bexhill when it was chased by a French vessel and subsequently seized and captured. However, the crew managed to escape before the French boarded her. Believing that they were about to take possession of a valuable cargo, they were surprised and disappointed when they boarded her to find that they had seized a cargo of stone. In order to quell their disappointment they took everything that was remotely of value from the vessel and cast it adrift. It was not long after this that a gale sprang up which drove the drifting vessel ashore where it became a total wreck at the hands of the ensuing stormy seas.

Margaret

Date sunk:	14.2.1813
Location:	Ashore at Rye
Type:	British sailing vessel
Voyage:	Lisbon to London
Master:	Downie
Ref:	SIBI V2 section 3

This vessel was driven ashore.

L'Rencon

Date sunk:	27.11.1814
Location:	Ashore at Rye
Type:	French galliot
Ref:	BPCP V4 p226

This French galliot, while off Rye, was caught in a severe storm during the morning of 27th November 1814. The crew had fought to bring the vessel under control, but in such terrible weather were always going to lose the battle against the elements. At 11am the vessel was driven ashore by the storm, but the crew were so exhausted from their endeavours to save the vessel that one by one they fell from the rigging into the raging sea and were drowned.

The people ashore, seeing the plight of the crew, managed to get a boat afloat in the most extreme of conditions and manoeuvred it to rescue the sole surviving member of the *L'Rencon*'s crew, a father of ten children.

Neptune

Date sunk:	27.11.1814
Location:	Off Hastings
Voyage:	Shoreham to Dieppe
No. of passengers:	18
Ref:	SWA 5.12.1814

This vessel left Shoreham at about 11am on Sunday 27th November 1814 bound for Dieppe. Among the 18 passengers was the widow, Mrs Jackson, whose husband had been this country's ambassador to America, accompanied by two female servants. Apart from Mrs Jackson there were also other wealthy passengers on board the *Neptune,* which resulted in there being a large amount of luggage cargo including Mrs Jackson's carriage on the vessel's deck. Also on board was a pack of foxhounds belonging to a nobleman, which were being taken to their owner who was in France, for hunting.

On leaving Shoreham, the *Neptune* made good speed in favourable conditions which unfortunately was to change when the vessel was about halfway across the Channel. It was then that the pleasant breeze rapidly changed to a south-westerly gale with accompanying heavy swell. The conditions got steadily worse with the waves breaking over the *Neptune*, putting the vessel's safety in some doubt. The vessel was eventually in such peril of sinking that it was decided by the ship's master that Mrs Jackson's carriage and the majority of the luggage cargo would have to be jettisoned overboard. It is in little doubt that had this not been done to make the vessel more buoyant, the *Neptune* would surely have sunk.

With the *Neptune* now a lot lighter, she weathered the storm but sustained sufficient damage to make it impossible, with an adverse wind, for the master to make for Dieppe and complete the voyage, or return to Shoreham. The vessel was now at the mercy of the weather and sea. Throughout that night and most of the following day she drifted ever nearer to Hastings where eventually she came to rest at about 4.30pm. The passengers, as well as the foxhounds, were all safely landed. The passengers were all taken to the Swan Inn and Cutter Inn to recover from their ordeal.

It was estimated that the financial loss to Mrs Jackson of her carriage, dresses and jewellery amounted to about £2,000.

Union

Date sunk:	4.12.1814
Location:	Rye Bay
Type:	French galliot
Cargo:	Wheat, flour
Home port:	Le Havre
Voyage:	Le Havre to London
Master:	Pain
No. of crew:	8
Ref:	SIBI V2 section 3; SWA 12.12.1814

This French vessel was driven ashore in terrible, rough weather near the entrance to Rye harbour at about 7am on Sunday 4th December 1814, having already sustained a leak to her hull while at sea. Due to the rough conditions, a boat could not be got out of the harbour to give assistance to the crew of the *Union*, who had taken to the rigging to prevent themselves from being washed overboard. However, after some considerable time had passed, a fishing boat managed to get out from the harbour and make for the stricken *Union*.

Due to the length of time, the crew dropped one by one from the rigging into the sea and drowned. They could not hold on any longer and had given in to sheer exhaustion. However, the mate was saved by the fishing boat and was brought ashore safely. It transpired that the mate was a married man with ten children and also had a financial interest in the vessel, which with its cargo was a total loss.

Margaret

Date sunk:	14.12.1816
Location:	Near Rye
Type:	British sailing vessel
Voyage:	Portsmouth to Sunderland
Master:	Brown
Ref:	SIBI V2 section 3

This vessel was driven ashore in a storm at the same time as the *Amalia*, (see page 37). All the crew were saved.

> ## *Amalia*
>
> **Date sunk:** 17.12.1816
> **Location:** Near Rye
> **Voyage:** Malta to Amsterdam
> **Master:** Bokin
> **Ref:** SIBI V2 section 3; SWA 23.12.1816

This vessel became stranded when driven ashore in the same storm as the *Margaret* on 14 December (see page 36). However, it appears not to have become a complete wreck until some three days later due to the constant action of the sea and weather. One of the crew and a small part of the cargo were saved.

On the same day that this vessel became a wreck, Tuesday 17th December 1816, a 70-year-old woman, Ms Bradley, was walking in a field at Rye when a bullock charged towards her. Unfortunately Ms Bradley was deaf and the number of people who were shouting at her of the impending danger were clearly not heard. When the bullock caught hold of her it threw her in the air and when she came down she fell onto the back of the animal. The bullock again tossed her into the air but on this occasion only a few feet or so. The animal then left her alone and miraculously it was found that she had not sustained any broken bones or any serious injury.

Mary

Date sunk:	13.10.1822
Location:	Near Hastings
Type:	British sailing vessel
Cargo:	Hops
Voyage:	Hastings to London
Ref:	SIBI V2 section 3

This vessel was driven ashore in a heavy gale.

Eagle

Date sunk: 1823
Type: Brig
Ref: BHB V2 p130

Friends of Liberty

Date sunk:	1824
Location:	Ashore at Hastings fish market
Gross tonnage:	40
Type:	British sloop
Date built:	1815, Rye
Owner:	C. Hicks
Master:	G. Rubie
Ref:	BHB V2 p111; SES p20; LR.1823.701(F)

Diligence

Date sunk: 22.12.1824
Location: Near The Priory, Hastings
Type: Sloop
Ref: BHB V2 p111

This sloop became a total loss just off The Priory at Hastings during a severe storm at high tide on 21st / 22nd December 1824, a storm which also claimed the *Sceptre* (see page 42).

The storm was reported to be so fierce that fishing boats on the beach at Hastings were hauled up into the High Street and All Saints Street for safety. A shop on the corner of Castle Street and Wellington Square, Hastings, was flooded with sea water which had managed to rise above the three steps at the front of the shop.

Sceptre

Date sunk: 22.12.1824
Location: Near Bexhill
Gross tonnage: 170
Type: Brig
Cargo: Silks, bullion, fruit
Ref: BHB V2 p111; BHB V3 p179

The *Sceptre*, like the *Diligence*, was driven ashore by the terrific storm that raged on the night of 21st/22nd December 1824. This particular vessel had some good fortune in that it was driven ashore when the tide was almost at its lowest. This resulted in the cargo being removed safely and the goods taken to Breed's warehouse in Hastings for storage. The bullion was taken to a local bank.

Active

Date sunk:	2.2.1825
Location:	Ashore at Hastings
Type:	Sloop
Home port:	Hastings
Owner:	Messrs James Breeds & Co.
Ref:	BHB V2 p111

On this particular night there was a terrific storm which caused damage to some Hastings vessels and totally wrecked others.

The height of the storm was between 10pm and midnight. There were five or six sloops on the beach at Hastings in extreme danger of being wrecked. Four of these sloops had already discharged their cargoes and one of them, the *Brunswick* of Rye, attempted to get off the beach through the raging surf. However, the vessel's hawser snapped and the boat was driven against two of the vessels still on the beach, namely the *Active* and the *Defence*. The damage caused by this collision meant that both became wrecks. The fourth sloop, the *Milward*, had not discharged its cargo of stone, which was still aboard. Like all the other vessels, she was being severely buffeted by the raging surf and sea. The *Milward* took such a battering that with its cargo still on board the vessel broke its back.

Defence

Date sunk:	2.2.1825
Location:	Ashore at Hastings
Gross tonnage:	79
Type:	Sloop
Home port:	Hastings
Date built:	1808, Hastings
Owner:	Messrs James Breeds & Co.
Master:	J. Brett
Ref:	BHB V2 p111; LR.1825.103(D)

See the *Active* on page 43 for details.

Brunswick

Date sunk:	2.2.1825
Location:	Ashore at Hastings
Gross tonnage:	52
Type:	Sloop
Home port:	Rye
Date built:	1823
Owner:	Stonham
Master:	W. Gains
Ref:	BHB V2 p111; LR.1825.651(B)

See the *Active* on page 43 for details.

Milward

Date sunk:	2.2.1825
Location:	Ashore at Hastings, near Ransom & Ridley's shipyard.
Type:	Sloop
Cargo:	Stone
Ref:	BHB V2 p111

See the *Active* on page 43 for details.

Albion

Date sunk:	1827
Location:	Ashore at Hastings
Cargo:	Silk, calico, rum, and general goods.
Home port:	Newcastle
Ref:	BHB V2 p112

This vessel caught fire while at sea and was abandoned by the crew. The cause of the fire is not known, but the vessel was taken in tow by other local vessels and brought to shore still ablaze. Once at the beach the local fire-engines extinguished the blaze and the greater part of the cargo was saved. It appears that many of the local inhabitants were sporting slightly burnt bandannas after this incident!

Rover

Date sunk:	1827
Location:	Ashore at St Leonards, opposite the Royal Victoria Hotel
Type:	Lugger
Ref:	BHB V2 p112

The *Rover* was driven ashore in a severe gale at what was then called Old Woman's Tap, where the following year the Royal Victoria Hotel was to be built. The master of the vessel unfortunately drowned.

William

Date sunk:	21.1.1827
Location:	Off Hastings
Type:	Fishing boat
Home port:	Hastings
No. of crew:	3
Ref:	BHB V2 p112

This fishing boat was caught in a sudden squall which caused her to sink with the loss of all three crew: George Morfee, Phillips and Bumstead. A fund for the families of these three men was set up and raised a total of £180.

It was reported that George Morfee's son later married a woman whose father also lost his life when crushed to death under a wagon. Fortunately these offspring lived until over 80 years of age, considerably longer than their parents.

Unknown

Date sunk:	25.11.1829
Location:	West of Camber Sands
Gross tonnage:	350
Type:	British cargo vessel
Cargo:	Oil, tobacco, cotton
Home port:	Liverpool
Voyage:	Liverpool to Breming
No. of crew:	14 and one boy
Ref:	SIBI V2 section 3; JRD

This vessel was lost in a terrible snowstorm off Camber Sands with the loss of all 14 hands and the ship's boy.

	La Constance
Date sunk:	19.1.1830
Type:	French Lugger
Voyage:	Treport to Dieppe
No. of crew:	10
Ref:	LL No. 6501 2.2.1830; RNLI

Gold medals were awarded to Lieutenant John Prattent, RN, and Lieutenant Horatio James, RN, for the rescue of nine of the crew of this vessel. Unfortunately, one man lost his life.

Fame

Date sunk:	1.2.1831
Location:	Ashore at Camber
Type:	British brig
Cargo:	Gold and silver ingots/bullion, raisins, almonds, olive oil
Voyage:	Messina to London
Master:	Shaxton
No. of crew:	8
Ref:	SIBI V2 section 3; JRD

This vessel ran ashore at about noon on 1st February 1831 in a very rough sea and a driving southerly snowstorm. It was probably the snowstorm and the obvious impaired visibility that caused the vessel to run ashore.

All eight hands were drowned, despite four heroic attempts by six coastguards together with five local fishermen to save them. Each of their four attempts was foiled by the vicious sea, terrible wind, sleet and snow. It was during the fourth attempt that the rescuers nearly became a casualty themselves, when the bottom of their boat was stove in, but they managed to get ashore safely. It was not until later when the tide had ebbed and the sea had subsided that they managed to reach the *Fame*, only to find two bodies of the original crew entangled in the vessel's rigging.

Two coastguard officers, Lieutenant Edward C. Earl, RN, and Lieutenant John Steane, RN, were later awarded gold medals for their leadership in trying to rescue this crew. The cargo of gold and silver ingots/bullion were in 11 boxes each containing £3,000 worth. However, only three boxes were recovered by the coastguard officers.

Betsey

Date sunk:	20.2.1831
Location:	Off Hastings
Type:	British sailing vessel
Voyage:	Ipswich to Liverpool
Master:	Riches
Ref:	SIBI V2 section 3

This vessel got into difficulties while off Hastings and managed to make contact with a passing ship, the *Columbia*, bound for New York. The *Columbia* took the crew off the *Betsey* and once they were all on board, the *Betsey* sank. Unfortunately one of the crew from the *Columbia* was drowned during the course of the rescue.

Hazard

Date sunk: 19.11.1831
Location: Mouth of Rye harbour
Type: British sailing vessel
Voyage: Newcastle upon Tyne to Sunderland
Master: March
Ref: SIBI V2 section 3; LL No. 6692 22.11.1831

This vessel had earlier been ashore at Dungeness and then moved a few miles west to finally sink at the mouth of Rye harbour. All the crew were saved.

L'Amiee

Date sunk:	21.11.1831
Location:	Ashore 1 mile (1.6km) from Rye harbour
Type:	French fishing lugger
Home port:	St Valery
No. of crew:	30
Ref:	LL No. 6692 22.11.1831; RNLI

The first anyone was aware that this French fishing lugger was in distress was at daybreak on Monday 21st November 1831, when she was found ashore in Rye bay, still flying the French flag. There was a raging storm at the time so when the alarm was raised the chief officer of the Rye coastguard station, Lieutenant Howard Parry, RN, gathered his men to assist in rescuing the crew. Their galley was brought half a mile over land to a point opposite the stricken vessel and launched with four coastguards on board.

The crew then set off for the *L'Amiee*. Over the course of four trips to the stricken vessel, a total of 21 men were brought to shore through the violent storm and raging seas. As a result of these four trips, the coastguard galley was so badly damaged that it was rendered unseaworthy. This left 10 men still on the *L'Amiee* who had to be brought ashore with the use of a rope.

Howard Parry was awarded a gold medal for the part he played in this rescue. It was noted that he had been a boy seaman at the Battle of Trafalgar.

Isabella

Date sunk:	20.2.1833
Location:	Wallsend, Pevensey Bay
Gross tonnage:	340
Type:	West Indiaman*
Cargo:	Plantation stores, brick ballast
Home port:	London
Voyage:	Gravesend to Demerara
Master:	James Wildgoose
No. of crew:	18
No. of passengers:	11
Ref:	SIBI V2 section 3; RS p326

The *Isabella* set sail from Gravesend, Kent, on Saturday 16th February 1833, with its passengers, their personal effects and cargo. By the early hours of the following Wednesday (20th February) she was just off Hastings and in a very severe storm. The storm drove the vessel towards the shore and at about 4am, with the tide being low, she hit rocks and ran aground about half a mile from the shore. As a consequence of hitting the rocks the vessel lost the use of her rudder, but the captain believed that he would still be able to refloat her by the use of the sails alone. However, he was not successful due to the heavy sea and the weather conditions. The captain's problems were further compounded because the vessel did not carry any flares, rockets or guns to warn the local coastguard of its predicament.

The sea and weather were buffeting the vessel with such force that the brick ballast in the hold was doing untold damage to the

---

*The term 'Indiaman' was first coined in the 16th century when Dutch East India Company (or VOC – Verenigde Oostindische Compagnie) built a number of ships for trade in the Dutch East Indies. However the company ceased in 1799, but the term for such ships carried on. Hence the term seemed to refer to a defensively armed, fully rigged, three masted merchantman with one or two decks, that normally plied the trade routes, for a number of northern European countries, between the Caribbean in the west (West Indiaman) and Asia in the east (East Indiaman).

hull. Each time the vessel rose and fell with the waves, the hull crashed onto the rocks on the outside, with the bricks smashing against it on the inside.

When daylight broke, the crew and passengers could see that a crowd had gathered on the beach, which raised their hopes and expectations of an early rescue, believing that the coastguard must now be aware of their situation. This was in fact the case: The Eastbourne lifeboat was being manhandled along the beach to a point opposite the stricken vessel, by 15 local fishermen, under the command of the lifeboat Coxswain, Edward Allchorn. Once opposite the *Isabella* the lifeboat was launched, but due to the extremely heavy surf the launch was not without difficulties. It took the Lifeboat crew a further 30 minutes to manoeuvre alongside the *Isabella*. Having come alongside, the lifeboat had to hold off due to the very bad sea conditions, but it stayed on station.

Meanwhile, on the *Isabella* herself, things were getting worse due to the combined effects of sea, wind and the brick ballast. The vessel was now taking in a lot of water and was clearly in imminent danger of becoming a total loss, with the potential risk of loss of lives. The ship's master, James Wildgoose, decided that he would let go another of the vessel's anchors in an attempt to turn the *Isabella* into the wind. The master was to some degree successful in that the anchor held and the vessel started to turn towards the wind. However, it was a painfully slow process and with the vessel taking on more and more water it was now getting heavier and reducing the effect of the master's efforts. By now the waves were washing straight across the vessel and the situation was becoming more desperate as each minute passed. Suddenly a huge wave pushed the *Isabella* further aground onto the rocks which, fortunately for all concerned, had a stabilising effect, making it much easier to get those on board off.

With the *Isabella* now much more stable than before, the lifeboat was able to come in closer. With this improved situation, Wildgoose tied a safety line between himself and the *Isabella* and jumped into the raging sea between the *Isabella* and the Lifeboat. He then got all the children on board passed to him one at a time so that he could hand them to the lifeboat crew through the surf. The women passengers followed next, followed, in true tradition, by the male passengers. This action by Wildgoose clearly saved all their lives. Once all 11 passengers were in the lifeboat, it returned to the shore with them and went back to the *Isabella* to collect the master and his crew. This process took a further two hours, with the lifeboat battling its way through the tremendous surf. Once ashore the passengers were taken by cart to local houses where they were all given dry, warm clothing.

Telemachus

Date sunk:	10.1.1834
Location:	East of Rye harbour
Gross tonnage:	124
Type:	British sailing vessel
Cargo:	Coal
Home port:	Rye
Date built:	1824, Sunderland
Owner:	Hammond
Master:	M. Hick
Ref:	SIBI V2 section 3; BHB V2 p113; LR.1833.61(T)

The *Telemachus* was driven ashore to the east of Rye harbour on the night of a terrific gale.

Conrad

Date sunk:	23.1.1834
Location:	6 miles (9.6km) east of Rye
Type:	Dutch brig
Cargo:	Blocks of tin
Voyage:	Batavia to Rotterdam
Master:	Scholborg
No. of crew:	11
Ref:	LL No. 6919 24.1.1834; LL No. 6920 28.1.1834; RNLI

When this vessel became a wreck near Rye on 23rd January 1834, Lieutenants Richard Morgan, RN and John Somerville, RN, together with 25 coastguards from the Rye coastguard station, waded into the raging surf and managed to get on board with ropes. The master and seven of the crew were safely taken to shore, but unfortunately the remainder were lost. Of the cargo, 141 blocks were saved. Morgan and Somerville were awarded silver medals for this rescue.

Hull Packet

Date sunk:	26.12.1834
Location:	Off Hastings
Type:	Steamer
Home port:	Sunderland
Date built:	1805
Ref:	SIBI V2 section 3; BHB V2 p113

Lord Exmouth

Date sunk:	18.1.1835
Location:	Near Brooks Watch House, Camber
Gross tonnage:	141
Type:	British brig
Cargo:	South African timber
Home port:	London
Voyage:	Sierra Leone to London
Date built:	1816
Owner:	J. Nixon
Master:	C. Gator
No. of crew:	9
Ref:	LR. 1834.443(L); JRD

The *Lord Exmouth*'s crew of nine were saved, but three monkeys that were on board were drowned. Shortly after this, a quantity of dollars and silver coins were found along the shore, which were assumed to have come from this vessel. They were still being discovered on the shore in April the following year.

On 27th January the *Lord Exmouth* was sold to the people of Lydd, Kent, for £101 which included the masts, bowsprit and the vessel's rigging. A week or so later, on 5th February, the vessel broke up and was subsequently resold at a considerable financial loss.

Collingwood

Date sunk:	11.4.1836
Location:	35 miles (56km) south east by south of Beachy Head
Voyage:	Newcastle to Gibraltar
Master:	Foster
Ref:	BHB V2 p134; LL No. 7151 15.4.1836

Fancy

Date sunk:	8.9.1838
Location:	Quarter mile (0.4km) south of Hastings
Length (feet/metres):	14/4
Home port:	Hastings
Voyage:	Local
Owner:	Robert Phillips
Master:	Robert Phillips
No. of crew:	1
No. of passengers:	2
Ref:	CPC 15.9.1838, 22.9.1838, 29.9.1838

At about 12 noon on this day, Robert Phillips was approached by a gentleman called Mr Moon and was asked if Phillips would take Moon out for a sail. It was agreed that they would set sail at 2pm that afternoon. A 12-year-old boy, George Erasmus Russell, who was a friend of Phillips, asked if he could also go with them, to which Phillips agreed as the boy had been to sea with him on previous occasions.

At the time they set off the wind was squally and northerly in direction which resulted in calm and flat water under the protection of the cliffs but a little more unsettled beyond the cliffs' protection. They set off east towards Lovers' Seat, with all three sails close-reefed. Phillips then tacked and started to return towards Hastings and sailed for 1½ miles (2km) close to the Castle Rocks. Here there was so little wind that he decided to reef the main sheet up and to get out the oars. Just as he was arranging this a slight breeze sprang up which allowed him to make a further tack. He had just completed this manoeuvre when a sudden strong gust of wind capsized the vessel before Phillips could get her under control or release the sheet. All three occupants were thrown into the sea. Phillips and Moon were both able to swim but the boy could not, and as the vessel was lying on its side at this stage he hung onto the mast. He worked his way along the mast until he reached the top, which suddenly went under the water. Phillips called out to Russell to let go of the mast. Russell said nothing and Phillips could only see Russell's hands scratching and struggling to keep hold of the mast as it disappeared under the sea.

A number of people on the shore had seen what had happened, and boats had been launched to assist the *Fancy*. Phillips and Moon had started swimming to the shore and when the rescue boats met up with them, Phillips told them to try and rescue the boy. However, the boats were to find no trace of Russell. The coastguard dragged for the boy's body for some considerable time, but without success. His body was later found on the morning of Tuesday 18th September 1838, some ten days after the incident, about 300 yards (274m) from the shore. The vessel was recovered a few days after this tragedy.

The coroner's inquest into the death of George Erasmus Russell was held at the South Saxon Hotel, Hastings, on Tuesday 25th September before the coroner, John G. Shorter Esq. During the course of the evidence heard, it was established that Phillips had been a mariner for 40 to 50 years and that Moon had been sailing on previous occasions but had little knowledge of boats. The coroner was satisfied that the vessel was properly ballasted and that this had not shifted in the hull. The jury returned a verdict of accidental death.

Louisa

Date sunk:	26.12.1838
Location:	Ashore at Hastings harbour
Type:	British schooner
Cargo:	Ballast
Home port:	Hastings
Owner:	Messrs Burfield
Master:	William Piper
Ref:	CPC 29.12.1838

The weather on the previous day, which was Christmas Day, had been quite pleasant but frosty, with the wind coming from the north. However, this changed at about 12 noon on Boxing Day with the wind swinging round to the south west, and growing all the time in ferocity until dusk, by which time the squalls were truly terrific.

On the shore at Hastings were four vessels: the *William Pitt*, the *Louisa*, the *Queen Victoria* and the *Sussex*. They had all discharged their cargo and taken on a further cargo bound for London. The storm was now at such a pitch that had these vessels not been loaded they would have been winched up the beach to beyond the waves and the surf. However, as this was not the case, the only option to save them from certain doom was to attempt to get the boats afloat. They were all successful in being hauled off the beach on the advancing tide, with the exception of the *William Pitt* which became waterlogged and was left to the mercy of the sea.

The *Sussex* was to the seaward of the *William Pitt* and the *Queen Victoria* and was trying to set sail when a combination of the wind and sea tore the jib off. This prevented the other two ships from carrying out a similar manoeuvre and they had to drop their anchors. There was now a real danger that these two vessels would be smashed against the rocks. The only option was to run for the shore which they did, but the conditions were such that there was a real possibility they would collide. However, due to the skill and seamanship of both crews this did not happen. Unfortunately the violence of the sea cast them onto the beach with tremendous force, resulting in the loss of the bowsprit and main top mast of the *Queen Victoria* and considerable damage to the *Louisa*. These two were now at the mercy of the weather and the turbulent sea, and the constant battering caused parts of the bulwark and rigging to be smashed and torn away.

The *Sussex* had by now dropped its anchor and was trying to sit out the storm. This it did until 8pm when it became apparent, with the ebbing tide, that if something was not done soon it would also be smashed against the rocks. It was decided to make a run for the beach. The anchor cable was cut and they managed to reach the beach near the eastern groyne. As soon as the vessel made the beach a wave struck it with such force that the boom was immediately broken off and carried away by the sea. The waves continued to break over the deck and the crew (which included a little boy), who were by now at the bow, were in imminent danger of being washed away.

This spectacle had drawn a large crowd. Fortunately there were many local seaman among the onlookers who linked arms and waded into the raging sea up to their chests to carry ropes to the crews of the stricken vessels. In so doing they were certainly putting their own lives at some risk, but due to their efforts all the crews got ashore safely.

William Pitt

Date sunk:	26.12.1838
Location:	Ashore at Hastings harbour
Gross tonnage:	38
Type:	British sloop
Cargo:	Iron, 65 quarters of oats and peas
Home port:	Hastings
Owner:	Messrs Burfield
Master:	J. Waters
Ref:	CPC 29.12.1838

See the *Louisa* on page 66 for details.

Sussex

Date sunk:	26.12.1838
Location:	Ashore at Hastings harbour
Type:	British sloop
Cargo:	160 quarters of oats and wheat
Home port:	Hastings
Owner:	Messrs J. Bailey & Co.
Ref:	CPC 29.12.1838

See the *Louisa* on page 66 for details.

Queen Victoria

Date sunk:	26.12.1838
Location:	Ashore at Hastings harbour
Gross tonnage:	99
Type:	British brig
Home port:	Hastings
Date built, builder:	1837, Messrs Ransom and Ridley
Owner:	T. Breeds & Co., Hastings
Master:	J. Young
Ref:	CPC 29.12.1838

See the *Louisa* on page 66 for details.

Les Trois Amis

Date sunk:	26.1.1840
Location:	West of St Leonards
Cargo:	Wine, brandy
Home port:	Dunkirk
No. of crew:	10
Ref:	LL No. 8077. 27.1.1840; BHB V1 p27; CPC 29.1.1840

In 1840 the weather started off in spectacular style with a succession of violent gales and storms between the 19th and 27th January. It was during this period, on Sunday 26th January, that one of these storms was accompanied by lightning and thunder of such severity that the ground shook. The storm caused widespread damage in Hastings, St Leonards and the surrounding area, including considerable damage to the sea wall at St Leonards.

The circumstances of how this vessel came to be a wreck are not really known other than it is believed to have capsized in a storm with the loss of all 10 hands, probably during the storm on 26th January. However, much was reported of the aftermath of its capsizing.

The first sighting of this vessel was at about 6am on the morning of Sunday 26th January, when *Les Trois Amis* was about a mile (1.6km) off Bexhill. It was bottom uppermost in the water and being washed towards the shore in a very turbulent sea. It finally reached the shore just to the west of St Leonards. Due to the position of the vessel in the water and to the buffeting it was taking from the sea, its mast and rigging were eventually smashed to pieces against the sea floor and the rocks. It was not only the mast and rigging that were torn from the vessel in this manner, but also the hold hatches. Once these had been smashed, the hold contents of casks of wine and brandy spilled out and were pushed to the shore by the waves.

It soon became local knowledge as to the contents of this vessel and before long there were hundreds of people on the beach, either to assist in recovering the casks or to watch those who were. One particular man who was trying to save a cask was so exhausted from fighting the surf that had he tried a few moments longer he would have been drowned. There were also men in groups of four or five trying to roll casks out of the surf. When they had managed to get them almost to the beach, along came a wave which washed both men and their cask back into the sea. Many of the casks were smashed open by the action of the sea throwing them onto the beach and many others were broken open by the people trying to rescue them, as refreshment! The smell of wine was on the air from St Leonards to Hastings.

With all this activity, Mr Gill of the customs, Mr Bevill the Lloyds agent and the coastal blockades men under the command of Captain Peat and Lieutenants Mann, Hire and Yule, RN, had great difficulty in protecting the vessel's cargo. Their work became even more difficult when night fell and a number of small groups managed to take away some of the casks. Some were even seen to take claret away in buckets or in a crock.

As the vessel was still bottom uppermost, an attempt during the evening was made to save the cargo still on the vessel by cutting a hole in the side of the hull, but this was without success. However, a further attempt was made the following morning when the remaining casks was successfully removed. Some of the casks, holding 200 gallons (900lit) each, had the merchant's name on them and 'Cette', which is a small port in the Gulf of Lyons. It was also found at this time that the cabins had all been knocked out by the movement of the cargo during the course of the ship becoming a wreck. It was also thought, however, that the cabins had been taken out deliberately so as to carry a greater cargo. If this was the case then the crew must have lived in a small roundhouse on the deck.

As the sea continued to pound the vessel over the next few days, the rigging and other parts of the vessel were slowly broken from her. Many of the locals swam out into the surf to rescue the various pieces.

James

Date sunk:	27.1.1842
Location:	Off Camber
Type:	British sailing sloop
Home port:	Hastings
Master:	Robert Phillips
No. of crew:	4
Ref:	SIBI V2 section 3; JRD; SE 5.2.1842

The night of Thursday 26th/Friday 27th January 1842 brought rough weather and heavy seas which would appear to have been the cause of the loss of this vessel. As far as is possible to ascertain, it seems that the *James* sank with the loss of all hands after the vessel's ballast shifted due to the sea conditions, while off Camber, Rye Bay. Those on board the *James*, apart from the Master, Robert Phillips, were Phillips' brother-in-law, Thomas Carpenter the mate, and three apprentices named Charles Sweetman, William Ball and Richard Wenman. Phillips left a wife and one child and the mate, Carpenter, left a wife and four children.

Once the vessel had settled on the seabed, several feet of the mast was visible above the sea at low tide. On Sunday 30th January 1842 an attempt was made to raise the *James* by two boats from Rye. However, this attempt was not very successful as they only managed to move the wreck several feet before abandoning it to the sea.

Singapore

Date sunk:	14.7.1844
Location:	4 miles (6km) east of Rye harbour
Gross tonnage:	302
Type:	Sailing barque
Cargo:	Timber
Home port:	Newcastle
Voyage:	Quebec to London
Master:	Simpson
No. of crew:	12
Ref:	SIBI V2 section 3; SWA 16.7.1844, 23.7.1844; SE 20.7.1844, 27.7.1844

This vessel became a wreck during the afternoon of Sunday 14th July 1844 when she was driven ashore in a south-westerly storm that was accompanied by ferocious seas. The crew had already left the *Singapore* in a longboat, but it had no oars which left it to the mercy of the sea. At 5am, a smack the *British Rover*, was fortunately close by and saw the plight of the crew. The master of the *British Rover*, James Bacon, took his boat among the surf at serious risk to both his own vessel and that of his crew. He got close to the drifting long boat, which was now in only 10 feet (3m) of water, and threw a line to them which they were able to catch. This then enabled the master and his 12 crew to be brought safely to shore, east of Dungeness. The rescued crew were then taken to the nearby Jolly Sailor Inn, kept by John Adames, arriving at about 1pm.

James Bacon was awarded a Silver Medal for this rescue.

The following Friday the salvaged parts of the *Singapore* and her broken hull were sold at auction and realised a total of £200. The cargo of 10,000 deals (planks of fir or pine) and 2,000 staves were salvaged and sent on to their original destination in London.

Kent

Date sunk:	30.7.1844
Location:	Ashore at St. Leonards
Type:	Collier
Owner:	Messrs Robert & Charles Deudney
Ref:	BMSS V3 p272

This vessel was ashore having discharged its cargo of coal for Mr Charles Deudney's warehouse at West Marina, when a fierce southerly gale blew up. The gale was at its height when the *Kent* attempted to get off the beach. During the attempt the hawsers broke resulting in the vessel being driven ashore, broadside on. The subsequent battering it took from the wind and the violent sea soon made the *Kent* a total wreck.

Once the vessel was on the beach, the crew were in imminent peril and had to get off as soon as possible. They managed to get ashore by means of a rope but had no time to save any of their clothing or belongings. The sum of £30 was later collected locally for the crew and distributed between them.

Mary Anne

Date sunk:	31.7.1844
Location:	Ashore Ness Point, Fairlight
Cargo:	Coal
Home port:	Hastings
Owner:	Messrs Harman & Co.
Master:	Freeman
Ref:	LL No.9482 1.8.1844; JRD; BMSS V3 p273; SE 3.8.1844

On the night of 30th July 1844 there was a terrific southerly storm and the *Mary Anne* was on the beach at West Marina, the same time as the *Kent*. Fortunately the *Mary Anne* did not suffer any material damage from the storm and was able to get afloat the following night. The weather had not subsided much by this time and a severe gale was still blowing. However, the success of getting afloat was to be short lived, because having got underway the vessel was soon driven ashore at Ness Point by the strong winds. All the crew were saved.

It is reported that the wreck was sold for £4.

It was only a few days prior to this event that the son of Mr Harman (owner of the *Mary Anne*), a lad of 11 years of age, was himself involved in a harrowing event ashore. It would seem that the boy was riding a horse along the High Street, Hastings, which was being led by another boy of about the same age. The horse suddenly bolted with Harman junior hanging on as much as his strength would allow. The horse was finally brought to a halt outside the Roebuck Inn by police Inspector Campbell, who managed to catch the bridle with one hand and the rider with the other!

Twee Cornelissen

Date sunk:	27.12.1845
Location:	Near Martello Tower No. 55, Pevensey Bay
Gross tonnage:	860
Length (feet/metres):	123.5/37.6
Beam (feet/metres):	22/6.7
Type:	East Indiaman
Cargo:	Coffee, sugar, indigo
Home port:	Amsterdam
Voyage:	Batavia to Amsterdam
Date built, builder:	1831, S.R. Boelen, De Haan, Amsterdam
Owner:	Harsten Bros & Co.
Master:	H.D. Van Wyck
No. of crew:	27
No. of passengers:	3
Ref:	SIBI V2 section 3; SWA 30.12. 1845; 13.1.1846; SE 3.1.1846; BHB V3 p278

It was about 1am on Saturday 27th December 1845 that tragedy struck this vessel. She had been 92 days out from Batavia for Amsterdam and at anchor waiting for a pilot in Pevensey Bay. It was while at anchor that a fierce south-westerly gale sprang up and, with the accompanying heavy seas, drove the vessel aground. It soon became apparent that the vessel would have to be abandoned, and 18 of the 31 people on board managed to reach the shore in the vessel's longboat.

The Eastbourne lifeboat, being aware of the plight of the *Twee Cornelissen*, was taken to Langney Point and launched under the command of Coxswain Samuel Knight at about 10.30am the following day, Sunday 28th December. However, before the lifeboat reached the *Twee Cornelissen* a small pleasure boat, the *Rebecca* had put off from Wallsend, Pevensey to try and assist. The boat was manned by Thomas Pierce and Thomas Woods, who were both pilots, and three coastguards: Oliver, Wornell and Flemming. Unfortunately they did not manage to get alongside the vessel before the lifeboat due to the terrible conditions.

On reaching the *Twee Cornelissen*, the lifeboat found that the remaining persons on board had taken to the rigging of the mizzen mast. This was the only place of safety as the huge waves were now breaking across her decks. Due to the conditions, Knight positioned the lifeboat to the stern and from this position managed to take off the captain and the rest of the crew who slid down a rope to the lifeboat.

When all were safely ashore it was noticed that one person was still hanging to the rigging. Those in the *Rebecca* checked the vessel but when they reached the *Twee Cornelissen* they found the man was already dead. The severe seas in the days following the incident completely broke up the vessel.

In recognition of the Eastbourne lifeboat's rescue, the entire lifeboat crew were presented with silver medals and certificates by the South Holland Lifeboat Society.

Henry

Date sunk:	7.7.1848
Location:	Off Fairlight
Type:	Sailing fishing lugger
Home port:	Hastings
Owner:	Philip Kent, Hastings
No. of crew:	2
Ref:	SIBI V2 section 3; SE 15.7.1848; HN 14.7.1848; BHB V3 p320

At about 1am on Friday 7th July 1848 the crew of the *Henry* (Mark White aged 58 and Joseph Swain aged 48) were fishing off Fairlight when they were run down by what was reported to be a large brig. The reason that it was thought to be a brig was because such a vessel had just left Rye harbour. The visibility at the time was said to be clear for about a mile.

Later the same day, about 3 miles (5km) off Fairlight, the masts and other equipment were found from the *Henry*. A few days later the vessel was raised and it was discovered that it had almost been sliced in two.

The body of Mark White was washed ashore two weeks later at Lydd, Kent, and was brought back to Hastings where he was buried at All Saints Church on 24th July. The body of Joseph Swain was never recovered. Both White and Swain were married men with children.

Whilst this book is not about fishing, 1848 was said to be the worst mackerel season for 20 years. However, it is interesting to note that the week preceding the loss of the *Henry*, a sturgeon was caught off Hastings weighing 68lbs (31kg) and measured 5 feet 10 inches (1.8m) in length. It was purchased by Mr T. Price, a local fishmonger from St Leonards, who sent the fish to London.

The loss of the *Henry*, like so many of the fishing vessels lost during this era, highlights the risk to the lives of fishermen especially at night with so many vessels passing up and down the coast. In fact it was recorded that on 20th December of the same year, after a period of particularly bad weather, that no fewer than 1000 vessels passed off Hastings.

Diana Grace

Date sunk:	11.1.1849
Location:	South west of Dungeness
Type:	British schooner
Cargo:	General goods
Home port:	Pwllheli
Voyage:	Liverpool to London
Master:	William Jones
Ref:	SE 20.1.1849; HN 19.1.1849; JRD

On the evening of Thursday 11th January 1849, the *Diana Grace* was seeking shelter to the east of Dungeness from a strong south-westerly gale. There were a number of other vessels also seeking refuge including the sloop, the *Phoenix* (see page 81), with a cargo of porter, spirits and timber for Hastings under its master, Thomas Palmer. The vessels were riding at anchor when at about 9pm the anchor cable of the *Phoenix* broke, allowing her to drift onto the schooner *Diana Grace*. The effect was devastating. No sooner had this collision occurred than the *Phoenix* quickly started to sink. The crew only just had enough time to get aboard the *Diana Grace* before the *Phoenix* sank. There was no time to collect any belongings.

In order to get clear of the sinking *Phoenix*, the master of the *Diana Grace* slipped anchor and was in the processes of getting the vessel's sails set when he went below and found the cabin full of water up to his knees. The water was entering the vessel at such an alarming rate that the crews of both vessels united to get the jolly boat ready. By the time the jolly boat was ready and the crews were aboard, the water was flush with the deck of the *Diana Grace*, which sank in about 15 fathoms of water.

The two crews drifted in their boat in a south-easterly direction at the mercy of the south-westerly gale until they were picked up by a French fishing boat which later put them ashore at Newhaven.

Phoenix

Date sunk:	11.1.1849
Location:	South west of Dungeness
Type:	British sailing sloop
Cargo:	Porter, spirits, timber
Home port:	London
Voyage:	London to Hastings
Owner:	Messrs J. & C. Burfield
Master:	Thomas Palmer
Ref:	HN 19.1.1849, 9.2.1849; JRD

See the *Diana Grace* on page 80 for details.

About three weeks after the *Phoenix* became a wreck, the vessel was raised and towed into Folkestone, Kent, where the cargo was discharged. It transpired that the vessel did not suffer too much damage and was repaired.

	Perseverance
Date sunk:	27.1.1849
Location:	Ashore opposite Saxon Hotel, Hastings
Gross tonnage:	97
Type:	British sailing schooner
Home port:	Hastings
Date built, builder:	1844, Messrs Lister & Bartram, Sunderland
Owner:	Messrs Putland, Winter & Chester
Ref:	LR. 1848.205(P); HN 2.2.1849, 16.2.1849

The *Perseverance* had been off Hastings for a few days, unable to come ashore due to the strong adverse winds that the area had been plagued with. However, on the morning of Saturday 27th January 1849, she finally got ashore and successfully discharged her cargo. By the time this had been completed and the ballast put on board ready to return to sea, it was late evening and the weather had deteriorated considerably. The wind had turned south westerly and by the time the *Perseverance* was ready to put to sea, it was described as hurricane strength.

With the deterioration in the weather, the sea became ever more rough and the waves more violent. At about midnight it was decided that an attempt would be made to float the vessel off the beach. Unfortunately during the course of getting her afloat part of the capstan broke, which left the vessel adrift. Inevitably she was smashed against a groyne. Those on the shore managed to get lines to the crew on board who got safely ashore through the vicious surf.

With the crew safely on dry land, a hawser was attached to the *Perseverance* and she was eventually hauled up the beach out of the sea. Only then was it discovered that she was repairable and the owners estimated it would take about two months to complete.

Lord Hill

Date sunk:	5.12.1849
Location:	Ashore at St Leonards
Cargo:	Stone
Voyage:	Caen to Hastings
Date built:	1810, Sunderland
Master:	Isaac Rose
Ref:	LL No. 11144 7.12.1849; HN 14.12.1849; BMSS V2 p224; HC 11.12.1849

This vessel arrived at St Leonards on 4th December 1849 with it cargo of stone blocks from Caen, France, for local Catholic church buildings. On the following day, with only part of her cargo discharged, she became the victim of a violent south-easterly storm. When the storm struck there were 51 stone blocks, each weighing 100 tons, still aboard.

The accompanying heavy seas washed over the vessel while it sat on the beach, resulting in the loss of the rudder, some hull planking and some starboard bulwarks. However, the vessel was still on the beach three days later on Friday 7th December, when the gale shifted direction to east-south-east. At about high tide it was found that somebody had unfastened the lashings which secured the hawser to the capstan. This allowed the *Lord Hill* to drift a short distance westward and lie broadside on the shore to the mercy of the waves. There were no reports of loss of lives.

There was much speculation after this incident that the proper equipment and correct personnel had not been involved in the discharging of the *Lord Hill*'s specialised cargo. It was felt that had such been used, then this accident would not have happened. However, the local authority was not empowered to insist that such equipment and personnel were used, with the result that unqualified people were employed, usually at a low charge, increasing the potential for accidents.

Scruger

Date sunk:	5.10.1850
Location:	Off Hastings
Length (feet/metres):	103/31
Beam (feet/metres):	23/7
Type:	British sailing schooner
Home port:	Shoreham
Date built, builder:	1848, James B. Bailey & Co., Shoreham
Master:	John Cobby
Ref:	SIBI V2 section 3

Owners Delight

Date sunk:	8.6.1851
Location:	Off Jury's Gap, 5 miles (8km) from Rye harbour
Length (feet/metres):	70–80/21–24 (Usually)
Type:	Billyboy (Liverpool barge)
Cargo:	Broken-up materials of a steamer
Home port:	Ipswich
Voyage:	Southampton to London
Date built:	1793, Bankside
Owner:	William Read
No. of crew:	3 and 2 boys
No. of passengers:	1
Ref:	SIBI V2 section 3; SE 14.6.1851; JRD; HC 17.6.1851

During the night of Sunday 8th June 1871, this barge sank during a heavy storm with the three crew, two boys and one woman, escaping in the vessel's jolly boat. They managed to row ashore to the east of Rye harbour near Dungeness.

Sally & Susannah

Date sunk:	6.8.1852
Location:	7 miles (11km) off Hastings
Type:	British sailing schooner
Home port:	Portsmouth
Voyage:	Hartlepool to Fareham
Date built:	1837
Owner:	Thomas Dyer, Southsea
Master:	Thomas Dyer
No. of crew:	4
Ref:	SIBI V2 section 3; HN 20.8.1852

At 2am on 6th August 1852, this vessel was involved in a collision with another schooner, the *Emma*, both from Portsmouth. At the time there was a force eight south westerly gale blowing. Fortunately all the crew were rescued by the *Emma* and later landed at Folkestone.

Sally

Date sunk:	12.11.1852
Location:	3–4 miles (5–6km) south by south-west of Hastings
Type:	British brigantine
Cargo:	Coal
Home port:	Sunderland
Voyage:	Sunderland to Fecamp
Date built:	1822
No. of crew:	5
Ref:	SIBI V2 section 3; SE 20.11.1852; HC 16.11.1852; HN 19.11.1852

During the night of Friday 12th November 1852, a fierce force ten easterly gale was blowing accompanied by torrential rain, and the captain of the *Sally* decided to seek shelter to the west of Dungeness. At about 11pm while the crew were preparing to anchor the vessel in order to weather the storm, the *Sally* collided with another brig, the *Unition* of Guernsey, also seeking refuge from the storm. The collision caused so much damage to the *Sally* that the crew decided it was unsafe to remain aboard. As a result, all the crew boarded the *Unition* and were safely landed the following day near Rye. The crew then walked into Rye town.

The *Sally* was now adrift without a crew on board, and at the mercy of the easterly gale. She finally sank at low water in about 14 feet (4m) of water off St Leonards, about six hours after the collision. It was not until daybreak that those ashore became aware of the events of the previous night because they could now see the masts protruding from the sea, some with the sails still set. As a result, a number of boats went out to the stricken vessel including the boat of the Priory coastguard, under the command of Lieutenant Coleman, in what was still a very turbulent sea. On arrival at the vessel they obviously found it deserted, not knowing the fate of the crew and that they were now safely at Rye. The *Sally* was still taking such a battering from the sea that at noon on Saturday 13th November the entire galley was washed off. This was brought ashore and the name *Sally* was found carved on the side of the galley.

It was clear that the *Sally* was not as badly damaged as the crew had initially thought. When the crew discovered this, they felt that they could have stayed on board and may have been able to put the vessel ashore safely. However, bearing in mind the conditions at the time, they were not to know how limited the damage was to be.

The vessel was owned by the master, who fortunately had it insured in Sunderland, but unfortunately the cargo was not insured. The wreck was later reported by Lieutenant Coleman to Trinity House, because it was now a danger to other shipping.

Good Intent

Date sunk:	23.11.1852
Location:	Rye harbour
Gross tonnage:	43
Type:	British barge
Cargo:	Timber
Home port:	London
Voyage:	Shoreham to Hastings
Date built:	1787
Master:	Samuel Hainsworth
No. of crew:	1
No. of passengers:	2
Ref:	SIBI V2 section 3; SE 4.12.1852; HN 3.12.1852; HC 30.11.1852

Samuel Hainsworth, his wife and their 5-year-old daughter, were aboard this vessel when a south-easterly force ten gale blew up. Hainsworth made a run for Rye harbour to seek protection from the weather but mistook 8 feet (2.5m) marker lights for 10 feet (3m) causing them to run aground on a sand bar. The vessel was at the mercy of the weather and the violent seas which were now washing over her. An hour and a half after having run aground, Hainsworth and his family were still aboard the *Good Intent* and being knocked about by the action of the sea on the vessel. Hainsworth was doing his best to protect them. He held his wife and put his daughter in his arms. They were in just such a position when they were all struck, either by the falling mast or by a piece of timber from the cargo which knocked Hainsworth's daughter out of his arms.

The crew of the Rye pilot galley were aware of their plight, so James Curd with George Rubie and three others set off in the galley and managed successfully to get alongside and take both Hainsworth and his wife off safely. The body of the child was later found in the fore hold having apparently been killed by the falling mast or timber.

Two days after this tragedy an inquest was held into the death of Hainsworth's daughter before a jury of residents from Winchelsea, which was presided over by the mayor, Mr R.C.N. Dawes. At the inquest Hainsworth said, *'I was then holding my wife and child, we all went down together and when I recovered my wife and I could not find my child.'* The jury returned a verdict of accidental death. The funeral of the young girl was conducted by the Rev. W.H.B. Churton, vicar of Icklesham, at the church of the Holy Spirit near the mouth of Rye harbour. This was the first ever funeral to be conducted at the church.

The master of this vessel was to have another accident at this very same spot 8 years later, on 7th June 1860. On this latter occasion Samuel Hainsworth was the master of a Thames sailing barge with a cargo of timber, bound for Le Havre when at high tide he ran aground.

Louisa Emilie

Date sunk:	27.12.1852
Location:	2 miles (3km) west of Dungeness
Cargo:	General
Home port:	Hamburg
Voyage:	Hamburg to Rio Grande
Master:	Carl Bartels
No. of crew:	10
No. of passengers:	72 (German emigrants)
Ref:	LL No. 12094 28.12.1852; JRD; SE 22.1.1853; HN 31.12.1853

As is the case with most shipwrecks, this vessel was caught in a severe storm with extremely vicious seas. Such was the violence of both weather and sea that she became a total wreck within 15 minutes of being blown ashore. This wreck stands out among many others because it had 72 German emigrants on board. Thirty-six of the 83 people aboard the *Louisa Emilie* were saved due to the heroic efforts of the local coastguard under the command of chief officer Brooks.

The vessel had come ashore in a violent storm and was among the boiling surf, making it impossible for the local coastguard to mount a rescue operation by boat. Chief officer Brooks together with his men and a local man called Clark Crosskey, set about trying to save as many of those on board as possible from the shore. Crosskey deserves a special mention as he managed to save six of those on board, which almost cost him his own life. He tied a rope around his body and, with a group of men holding the other end, repeatedly plunged into the boiling sea and swam to the stricken vessel. He was then hauled to shore with those he had rescued. However, on his last attempt and now feeling totally exhausted, he was struck by a particularly large wave that knocked him unconscious. The beach party, when they hauled him ashore, were very concerned for his well-being, but fortunately he recovered.

There was a total loss of 46 lives from this vessel, including the master, Carl Bartels, the second mate and three seamen. The master stayed on the vessel throughout the ordeal and was killed not by drowning but by falling timber from the vessel.

Those who witnessed these events reported them as most heart-rending, with people totally distraught at the loss of their families. There were children sobbing for their missing parents, wives and husbands without their partner, two fathers each holding a child, one as young as 9 months, and one woman with a child under each arm who had been thrown ashore by the waves.

The survivors of this wreck were taken to Lydd where the local people cared for them as best as they could, providing clothes and other essentials.

On 12th January 1853, two men and four orphans of the emigrant survivors left Lydd in the company of the vessel's mate, Jacob Dierks, and returned to Hamburg. The remaining survivors left for Portsmouth to continue their voyage to Brazil. However, before they left they were given money that had been collected from local people. The allocation of these funds was decided at Lydd, on 12th January by a committee chaired by the vicar of Lydd, Rev. R. Smith. The money collected amounted to £365.10s.8½d and was allotted by the committee as follows:

	£.	s.	d.
Licht, widow	10	17	6
Schutz, two brothers	21	15	0
Wagner, widow	14	17	6
Wagner, two brothers, boys	14	10	0
Wagner, young woman	10	17	6
Gravender, man, wife and boy	29	0	0
Johan, man, wife and infant	25	7	6
Johan, man and boy	18	2	6
Johan, young man	10	17	6
Wachter, man and infant	18	2	6
Steiger, four children, orphans	36	5	0
Nasbaummer, and child	18	2	6
Charles Volkhart	10	17	6
Ferdinand Volkhart ⎫	10	17	6
Arnold Volkhart ⎬ young men	10	17	6
Heinrich Volkhart ⎭	10	17	6
Teltscher, widow and daughter	25	7	6

Edmond Teltscher, young man	10	17	6
Rudolph Teltscher, young man	10	17	6
Ferdinand Greiner, young man	10	17	6
Otto Reimanus	10	17	6
Jacob Dierks, mate of vessel, who aided in saving many lives	10	17	6
Gratuities to the children		11	0
For the purchase of extra provisions at sea	10	0	0
Balances for boxes for emigrants and expenses	6	11	8½
	£365	10	8½

Regina

Date sunk:	15.1.1853
Location:	Off Hastings
Type:	Snow
Home port:	Liverpool
Voyage:	London to Smyrna
Date built:	1846, at Sunderland
Owner:	Messrs Campbell
Master:	Wakeham
No. of crew:	11
Ref:	SIBI V2 section 3

This vessel was travelling along the English Channel off Hastings in a force nine south-westerly gale when it collided with an unknown vessel and sank. It appears the crew were all saved by the Kingsdown lifeboat from St Margaret's Bay, Kent. The vessel was valued at about £800 but had been insured for £1320.

Kingston by Sea

Date sunk:	1.10.1853
Location:	8 miles (13km) off Hastings
Length (feet/metres):	78/24
Beam (feet/metres):	21/6
Type:	British sailing brigantine
Cargo:	200 tons of coal
Home port:	Shoreham
Voyage:	Hartlepool to Shoreham
Date built:	1843, at Sunderland
Owner:	George Glasebrook
Master:	Thomas Glasebrook
No. of crew:	9
Ref:	SIBI V2 section 3; HN 7.10.1853; SE 8.10.1853

At about 3am on Saturday 1st October 1853, the brig *Kingston By Sea* was bound for her home port of Shoreham with a cargo of coal. The vessel was about 10 miles (16km) south-west of Hastings on a very dark night but in fine weather and with a good sailing breeze. The ship was making good headway in this breeze when an unknown full-rigged ship ran her down. This collision caused the *Kingston By Sea* to sustain severe damage to her hull, resulting in water entering the vessel where members of the crew including Thomas Morley, a 20-year-old from Fulling. Morley immediately made his way from below decks to the hatchway and as he was going through he was fatally struck by the falling fore mast. With Morley's body now blocking the hatchway, the other crew members still below decks could not get out. They had to go to the fore hatch and fortunately managed to release it and get out onto the deck.

The ship's master, Thomas Glasebrook, called out to the unknown vessel for assistance because his vessel was sinking. The unknown ship gave the incredible reply that they had no boat to hand and kept sailing on without offering any help at all.

The fallen fore mast had caused such damage to the vessel that the crew were left with no option but to cut away the main mast and throw both masts overboard together with all the rigging, leaving a clear deck. This of course left the vessel drifting helplessly and with water entering rapidly, the crew had to man the pumps in order to keep afloat.

At about 6am the *Rio de Janeiro* of Cowes came on the scene and took the vessel in tow. After three hours of being under tow, and now 8 miles (13km) off Hastings, the wind started to increase in strength. The *Kingston By Sea* was taking in more and more water and it was decided that she should be abandoned. Having made this decision the crew safely transferred onto the *Rio de Janeiro* with the master being the last to leave. He had only just got on board when the *Kingston By Sea* went down, taking the corpse of Thomas Morley with her.

The surviving crew were later landed at Dungeness and travelled by train to Hastings, arriving in the afternoon. They stayed the night at Hastings before continuing their train journey the following morning to Shoreham.

John Weavel

Date sunk:	4.10.1853
Location:	Sea wall near Eversfield House, St Leonards
Gross tonnage:	107
Type:	Collier schooner
Cargo:	Coal
Home port:	Hastings
Voyage:	Shoreham to Hastings
Owner:	Messrs H. Tree & Co.
No. of crew:	6
Ref:	SIBI V2 section 3; SE 8.10.1853; HN 7.10.1853

This North American vessel, built of fir, was on the slipway at St Leonards on the morning of Tuesday 4th October 1853, having just discharged its cargo of coal. It was high tide and, with the sea very rough indeed and getting worse all the time, it was decided to try and get the vessel afloat. All those involved made great efforts to achieve this but due to the sea conditions their efforts resulted in the moorings being pulled up and some of the vessel's tackle giving way. This left the vessel at the mercy of the sea and being driven onto the adjacent groyne. Those ashore pulled the crew through the raging surf by ropes attached to the vessel. By now the sea was breaking furiously over the stricken boat with such force that the *John Weavel* was forced through the groyne and driven up against the sea wall in front of Eversfield House. The crew lost all their possessions including the master's instruments.

At about 12.45pm that afternoon the vessel was split across the middle. The masts had broken and the effect of the constant battering by the sea broke the vessel into so many small pieces that it soon totally disappeared. The vessel's provisions were later seen floating in the sea, and the local police did all they could to prevent them being stolen by the hundreds of spectators who arrived to witness the events.

Anna

Date sunk:	24.1.1854
Location:	Hooks Point, 3 miles (5km) east of Hastings
Type:	British sloop
Cargo:	Pipe clay, paper
Home port:	Poole
Voyage:	Poole to London
Master:	Hescrof
No. of crew:	3
Ref:	SIBI V2 section 3; HC 25.1.1854

This vessel was in collision with the Danish brig, *Gloria Deo*, when approximately 3 miles (5km) east of Hastings in a force eight storm. The crew were all saved by the *Gloria Deo* and later put ashore at Portsmouth.

Notre Dame de Mont Carmel

Date sunk:	1.1.1855
Location:	Near Rye harbour
Type:	French sailing lugger
Home port:	Treport
Master:	Brunet
No. of crew:	2 and 1 boy
Ref:	SIBI V2 section 3; SE 6.1.1855

At about 11am on New Year's Day 1855, there was a north-westerly force eight storm blowing in Rye Bay. The *Notre Dame de Mont Carmel* was running for Rye Harbour to seek shelter from the storm. On entering the harbour the vessel struck a stone pier and sank almost immediately. Two of the crew were saved by two local men in their boat but unfortunately the vessel's boy, Eustance Lemoin, was washed overboard and drowned.

Lemoin's body was recovered and an inquest was held into his death on the following Wednesday before the coroner and deputy mayor of Winchelsea, Mr C. Robbins. A verdict of accidental drowning was recorded and the boy's body was buried the next day at the church of the Holy Spirit, Rye Harbour.

John & Mary

Date sunk:	27.9.1856
Location:	2 miles (3km) west of Rye
Type:	British sailing sloop
Cargo:	Stone
Home port:	Sunderland
Voyage:	Caen to London
Date built:	1838
Owner:	John Hodgson
Master:	John Hodgson
No. of crew:	2
No. of passengers:	5
Ref:	SIBI V2 section 3; SE 4.10.1856; HN 3.10.1856

At about 10am on the morning of Saturday 27th September 1856, this vessel was caught in a force ten southerly storm. It was one of the fiercest southerly storms the Channel had experienced for many years.

The vessel had loaded its cargo of stone at Caen, France, the previous day, bound for London. Those on board, apart from the master, mate and one seaman, were the master's wife and his four children – two sons aged 18 and 14 and two daughters aged 16 and 12.

The master had kept the vessel in mid-Channel to avoid any problems with either the French or English coasts and to ensure she had plenty of sea depth beneath her, bearing in mind the cargo. Due to its barge-like construction, when the storm struck it was almost impossible for the master to steer the vessel into the storm to keep it away from the English coast. This meant that the *John & Mary* was driven nearer and nearer to the coast. Eventually she lost both jib and foresail in the ferocious gale and she was finally driven ashore near Cliff End. With the vessel now ashore, the waves continued to sweep across the decks and before the master's wife and three of his children could lash themselves to the rigging, they were washed overboard and drowned. The fourth and eldest of the children was later found drowned, still in the vessel's cabin. The master, John Hodgson, John Wellborn the mate and seaman Charles Shippington were able to lash themselves securely to the rigging. The coastguards William Smith, John Tremble, Thomas Talbot and William Shepherd under the command of Lieutenant Roe (Haddocks coastguard station) and Lieutenant Farrer finally rescued them, using a lifeline once the tide had receded sufficiently for this to be done safely in the surf.

The body of the eldest girl, Mary, aged 16 years, was soon found. The body of the master's 14-year-old son William was found in Rye harbour about 5am the following morning. On Monday 29th September, the inquest into the death of William was held at the Ship Inn, Icklesham, before the coroner, Charles Robins, who was also the mayor of Winchelsea. The inquest heard evidence both from John Iggleden who was with his son when he found the deceased's body in Rye harbour, and from the vessel's mate. The master was too distraught to attend and give evidence.

The following day, Tuesday 30th September, saw the inquest of Mary Hodgson take place at the Ship, Pett, before the coroner for the Rape of Hastings (the county of Sussex was divided into six divisions, each called a Rape), Mr N.P. Kell. The first to give evidence was the seaman Charles Shippington, who came from Driffield in Yorkshire. He gave evidence of identification of Mary and told of the last hours of the vessel. The next witness was George Tegg, a boatman with the coastguard, who told the Inquest that at 1pm he waded out to the *John & Mary* when the tide had receded, and searched the cabin area of the vessel which was smashed to pieces. He had been searching in the debris for about 20 minutes when he found the body of the deceased Mary, under a partition deck. The verdict at both inquests was that the children accidentally drowned.

The funeral of both children took place on the afternoon of Wednesday 1st October at the church of the Holy Spirit at Rye Harbour, officiated by Rev. H.B.N. Churton, vicar of Icklesham.

Draper

Date sunk:	7.10.1857
Location:	Rock-a-Nore, Hastings
Gross tonnage:	67
Type:	British sailing sloop
Cargo:	86 tons of coal and 233 pieces of machinery
Home port:	Plymouth
Voyage:	Newcastle to Falmouth
Date built:	1812
Master:	Thomas Pierce
No. of crew:	3 and a boy
Ref:	SIBI V2 section 3; LL No. 13579. 9.10.1857; BMSS V6 p221; HN 9.10.1857; SE 10.10.1857; HC 14.10.1857

The *Draper* left Newcastle on 28th September 1857 bound for Falmouth. The people of Hastings first became aware that the vessel was in distress at 9.15pm when a local coastguard fired his pistol. This attracted many spectators who came to watch the unfolding drama.

The vessel and its crew of four were being driven by the violent storm that was raging at the time, not far from the beach. It was low tide and there was a very strong surf which made the sea foam for as far as the eye could see. The *Draper* was forced by the weather onto the rocks at the Rock-a-Nore groyne. In order to effect some form of rescue, the launch of a large ferryboat was attempted, with the help of horses from the beach. However, the surf and weather were such that this endeavour was totally unsuccessful as there was no possible chance of rowing the ferryboat out of the surf. The only possible option to save the crew would be a mortar and line, but the nearest was at St Leonards. On the beach at the time was a local youth named Enefer who was an exceptional swimmer. He tied a rope around himself and dived into the surf. He almost reached the stricken vessel but was clearly very exhausted, so those ashore hauled him back. They found that the rope had got around his neck and it was obvious he was in severe danger of losing his own life.

One or two of the crew could be seen from the shore lashed to the mast but every wave that struck the vessel threw her on her beam ends and washed over the boat and the crew. At times the mast was totally under the sea.

The vessel, having been blown onto the rocks, soon became a total wreck with the loss of all the crew.

When pieces of timber were later recovered from the wreck, it was found that they were mostly rotten, which tends to suggest that the vessel was not in a seaworthy condition at the start of her voyage. This event caused one local fisherman to say, *'If any vessel in a heavy sou'wester misses the mouth of the harbour and runs on dem'ere rocks woe betide the crew; never a man will come out alive.'*

Pilgrim

Date sunk:	8.10.1857
Location:	Opposite Albion Hotel, Hastings
Gross tonnage:	181
Type:	British snow
Cargo:	Coal
Home port:	Middlesbrough
Voyage:	Not known to Portsmouth
Date built:	1842
Owner:	Messrs Smith & Comper, Gosport
Master:	Smithson
No. of crew:	8
Ref:	LR. 1857.289 (P); HC 14.10.1857

At 7am on Thursday 8th October 1857 in an extremely strong gale, the *Pilgrim* ran aground on a sandbar immediately in front of the Albion Hotel, Hastings. Fortunately for all concerned, the tide was halfway, which ensured the vessel was clear of the turbulent sea.

The first boat launched to rescue the crew was a local lifeboat belonging to John Wright who was accompanied by four coastguards, namely, James Harris, George Goodman, John Gilliard and John Pratt. Soon after they were afloat the town lifeboat was also put to sea and made for the stricken *Pilgrim*.

The town lifeboat was the first to reach the ship, only to find she was rapidly filling with water. Five of the *Pilgrim's* crew, namely Robert Hammond (mate), Arthur Trimmell junior, Stephen Gardner, George Martin and Henry Wright, were safely transferred to the lifeboat and carried back to shore where they were met by the deputy mayor J.C. Burrows, and the local chief officer of police, Mr Duly, together with a number of his men. The remainder of the *Pilgrim's* crew, which consisted of Smithson (master), Arthur Trimmel senior and Douglas Dent, remained on board until John Wright's lifeboat came alongside. They also were successfully transferred into the lifeboat and returned safely to shore.

The rescued crew were all taken to the Wellington Inn where they had breakfast. After this they went to the town hall and were fitted out with clothing purchased for them by the deputy mayor and Mr Duly. The deputy mayor found beds for the crew at the Cricketers' Inn, also at his own expense. The crew were well received and one act of sympathy, among many, shown towards them was that of a lady who watched the events unfold and, upon being told that the crew were safe, gave £5 towards their relief.

The deputy mayor, when he next sat on the local magistrates' bench, took the opportunity to thank the chief officer of police and his officers and commended the actions of John Wright and the crew of his lifeboat. He also announced that contributions towards the crew's relief could be made either to local banks or direct to himself. A Mr Scott, an accompanying magistrate, opened the relief fund by donating a sovereign.

The crew of John Wright's lifeboat were his son (also called John), John Stoner, James Ashurst, John Spicer and Charles Marchant. The crew of the town's lifeboat were Nathaniel Gunn, Frederick Collins, John Taylor, William Measer, Thomas Ashurst, Thomas Care and Walter Coates.

Coastguard vessel (unnamed)

Date sunk: 17.1.1859
Location: Off Pevensey
Type: Four-oared galley
Owner: Pevensey coastguard station
Master: Dennis Perrin
No. of crew: 5
Ref: HC 19.1.1859; HN 21.1.1859, 28.1.1859

This is a story where the rescuers themselves needed to be rescued. This four-oared galley belonged to Pevensey coastguard station and at the time of the unfortunate event was ferrying some old flags and pennants from the coastguard station to a coastguard cutter named the *Active*.

The chief officer of the station, Lieutenant Mansel, had given orders the previous evening that, once the *Active* came into view, the station's galley was to put to sea with its cargo of flags and pennants and take them to the *Active*. On the morning of Monday 17th January at 10am, Michael Russell of the coastguard station was the first to see the *Active*. At the time there was a violent sea running and the tide was ebbing. At about 12.45pm, when the *Active* was almost a mile (1.6km) off the shore, the coastguard vessel finally set off for the cutter. The crew consisted of Perrin (acting as coxswain), William Hutchings, William Bricknell, William Cook and Michael Russell.

There was a stiff breeze blowing which was freshening all the time. The vessel got alongside the *Active* without any great difficulty and the cargo of flags was put aboard. The coastguard vessel then made to return to the shore. Perrin appeared to have the vessel under control until it reached the breaking waves and surf. Then, instead of waiting for a calm patch of sea after the 'third wave' and running the boat in stern first, he kept it bow first into the surf. The vessel suddenly broached, throwing most of the crew into the sea. Three of them managed to hang onto the stern. The vessel was now filling with water but was still afloat and drifting eastwards. Lieutenant Mansel realised that this could be a potential disaster and so sent a member of his detachment, William Dent, to fetch the coastguard's chief boatman and his boat. However, the chief boatman, named Munday, would not launch the boat because it was impossible to get her through the sea, especially as the vessel in distress was much the same type of boat.

By coincidence, Dent should have been one of the crew of the galley but was five minutes late arriving and so missed the launch. Michael Russell went in his place.

Mansel, having given this order to Dent, stripped off and headed into the sea with the intention of saving the vessel's crew. He managed to get hold of the only survivor, Michael Russell, who was floating quite close to the shore, and haul him to safety.

Three of the dead crewmen had families. Perrin and Cook both had five children all under 15 years of age, with Cook's youngest only being 8 weeks' old. Hutchings was also married with five children.

Cook's body was found at low water by James Balcombe, a labourer employed by Major Vidler, a local surveyor, at about 5pm the same day. As a result an inquest into his death was held at the Sluice Inn, Pevensey, before Hastings borough coroner Mr R. Growse and a jury. Captain Gough, RN, Commander of the coastguard district, attended as an observer. The rescued man, Russell, did not attend the hearing as he was still too unwell to give evidence.

During the hearing Lieutenant Mansel said that he had been in the service nearly two years and had been stationed at Pevensey for about eight months. In his evidence to the coroner he said that he did not think it was too rough to send the boat out, although he had not sent it out before except for the one occasion he himself went out in it. Under questioning Mansel said that the crew did not practise at the station and that they had not been out on exercise since he had been there. Although the chief boatman, had been at the station for seven years, Mansel considered his own judgement and knowledge of the sea to be superior to his. He accepted that none of the crew had been provided with cork jackets or lifebelts. The coroner felt that had the crew been provided with these there may well not have been loss of life. He told the jury that there was no doubt that Cook's death had been caused by accidental drowning but it was for them to decide whether there was any criminal conduct on the part of Lieutenant Mansel, even though the coroner believed there was none. If there was any misconduct on his behalf, then it was for his senior officers to take the necessary action.

The jury agreed with the coroner and formally returned a verdict of accidental drowning. They also made the recommendation that the coastguard should be provided with the proper life-saving equipment when going to sea in rough conditions and that the gallant conduct of Lieutenant Mansel after the tragedy be brought to the attention of his senior officers.

On Saturday 22nd January the body of Hutchings was found among the rocks opposite Hastings fishmarket by a youth named Chatfield, who was searching for whelks at low tide. The body was embedded in the sand, face down, with only part of the legs and heels showing above the surface. The body of Perrin was found the same day near Galley Hill. The inquest into the death of Perrin was held at the Bell Inn, Bexhill, before Mr N.P. Kell, the coroner for the Rape of Hastings.

At this hearing the rescued man, Russell, was fit enough to attend and give evidence. He said that he had two war medals, one for the coast of Syria and the other for the Baltic. He said that once the boat had broached he was thrown into the sea. When he had recovered himself he found he had an oar in his hand which he handed out to Perrin who was still in the waterlogged boat. He asked Perrin to pull him aboard, but before he could do this a wave washed him away from the boat. He said that he also found one of the seats from the vessel, and with the oar he had swum for the beach to be met by Lieutenant Mansel. He said that he was so exhausted that had Mansel not been there then he would surely have drowned. Once the sea washed him away from the vessel he did not see any of the crew again. Although he had not been out in such a boat as this in such rough weather he did not object to doing so. He had been in similar seas in the West Indies but had been in eight- and ten-oared boats.

Harbinger

Date sunk:	2.9.1859
Location:	Ashore at Hastings
Type:	Schooner
Cargo:	160 tons of coal
Voyage:	Seaham to Hastings
Owner:	Messrs Kent
Master:	Clifton
Ref:	BHB V3 p185; HN 9.9.1859

The North American vessel arrived off Hastings during the morning of Friday 2nd September 1859 with its cargo of 160 tons of coal, in what was ever-worsening weather. During the afternoon the vessel's owners decided that they would beach the vessel in order to discharge its cargo and ballast. It was not until midnight that the vessel was ready to sail again, by which time the weather had turned into a violent storm. The arrangement made to get such vessels afloat was by the use of two hawsers attached to the stern, to pull the vessel off the beach. By the time this operation was ready the storm was at its height. The force of the weather and sea against the hawsers was such that one of the hawsers snapped under the strain. This caused the second hawser to snap too due to the added strain on it.

Without hawsers there was now no way to control the vessel from the stern, which resulted in the sea turning it broadside-on and driving it ashore. An attempt was made to hold her fast from the bow by chains and warps attached to the capstans. This was successful for a period of time, but in the end even this was not sufficient to beat the ever-increasing weather and sea. Inevitably the chains broke away and the vessel drifted towards Mercer's Bank where it heeled over to seaward. It was now abundantly clear to the lifeboat coxswain, Mr Morfee, that the vessel was in a hopeless position and so with the aid of lifelines he managed to get the crew safely ashore.

During the night the wind changed direction from south east to north east, causing a very heavy sea. This meant the vessel received a very heavy pounding from the changed sea conditions, which finally caused the decks to collapse. This together with a receding tide, put so much strain on the ship's keel that it forced the timbers apart, making the vessel a total loss.

The estimated value of the *Harbinger* was £400, of which about £100 was to be recovered from the actual value of the wreck. The remaining £300 was suffered as a loss by the owners because vessels that were beached in order to discharge their cargo were not insurable.

Fortunately there was only one injury sustained during this wreck, and not serious: a capstan spar hit a man when the initial stern hawser snapped.

It is believed that had the *Harbinger* been ready to sail about 30 minutes or so earlier, she would have successfully got clear of the beach and been safe.

Canton

Date sunk:	4.12.1859
Location:	Near Camber coastguard station
Gross tonnage:	500
Type:	Swedish sailing barque.
Cargo:	Hides, rice, saltpetre
Voyage:	Calcutta to London
Date built:	c. 1855
Owner:	Westerwyk
Master:	Niels Olsen
No. of crew:	17
Ref:	SIBI V2 section 3; LL No. 14249. 5.12.1859; HC 7.12.1859, 14.12.1859; HN 9.12.1859; SE 10.12.1859

The cause of this wreck was due to a navigation error by the pilot and crew. The vessel was *en route* to London from Calcutta but had put in at Cowes on the Isle of Wight to take on board a pilot and new sails. The *Canton* then continued its voyage to London where, at about 4am on Sunday 4th December 1859, she found herself in heavy south-westerly gale to the west of Dungeness. On seeing the Dungeness light, the pilot and crew mistook it for one on the French coast. The crew, in this belief, then steered more northerly of the light which resulted in the vessel running aground near Camber coastguard station. As soon as the vessel ran aground it immediately began to break up. This unfortunately caused the loss of the lives of 13 of the crew, the master and the pilot. One of the crew was a man from Dover who had joined the vessel at the start of its voyage in Calcutta. Two of the crew, Lars Olsen and Samuel Oberg, managed to survive by clinging to part of the wreckage and were washed ashore near Jury's Gap coastguard station.

The terrifically heavy seas soon smashed the vessel to many pieces, so much so that bow was found ¼ mile (400m) away from the stern section and masts.

Apart from the humans on board there were also a dog and a

pig. It is strange, but it appears that the dog drowned whereas the pig managed to reach the shore alive and was taken to nearby Broomhill.

Carnanton

Date sunk:	5.12.1859
Location:	Near Martello Tower No. 36
Gross tonnage:	86
Type:	British schooner
Cargo:	Silver sand
Home port:	Llanelly
Voyage:	Rouen to Gloucester
Date built:	1841, Llanelly
Owner:	Brabyn & Co.
Master:	Nicholas Brabyn
No. of crew:	4
Ref:	LR. 1859.125(C); HC 14.12.1859; HN 9.12.1859; SE 10.12.1859

This was the second vessel to become a wreck within two days. The first was the *Canton* (see page 111) and the second was the *Carnanton* at about 9.30pm on Monday 5th December 1859. The *Carnanton* was further west along the coast, near Pett.

The vessel suddenly sprang a leak. The crew manned the pumps to try and stem the flow of water. However, the pumps became choked and seeing that the vessel was quickly filling with water, they took to their boat. The *Carnanton* was left to drift and eventually ran aground near to Martello Tower 36. The crew's ordeal was not over once in the vessel's jolly boat, because as it came through the foaming surf it capsized, throwing the crew into the sea.

Fortunately for the crew, the local coastguard were already aware of the plight of the *Carnanton* and were making plans to rescue the crew. It was due to the efforts of coastguardsmen William Smith (chief boatman), John Campbell, David Burgess and George Well, attached to the Martello Tower 36 station, and that of Joseph Snook of the Haddocks station, that the crew of the *Carnanton* were safely brought to shore.

The following Friday night, the vessel was refloated and arrived at Hastings in the morning with six feet (1.8m) of water in her hold.

Perseverance

Date sunk:	17.4.1860
Location:	Ashore at Rye
Type:	British sailing smack
Cargo:	Chalk
Home port:	Rye
Voyage:	Rye to Holywell
Master:	Fuller
Ref:	SIBI V2 section 3

This vessel became a wreck while about to embark on a voyage from Rye to Holywell with its cargo of chalk. The vessel was still on the beach and being constantly buffeted by a heavy surf which caused it to become a total wreck before it could get clear of the beach and set sail on its journey.

Georgiana

Date sunk:	2.6.1860
Location:	Off Rye harbour
Type:	British sailing schooner
Cargo:	Bricks
Home port:	Whitby
Voyage:	Faversham to Dungeness
Ref:	SIBI V2 section 3; SE 5.6.1860; HC 6.6.1860, 13.6.1860; RNLI

This vessel was at anchor off Rye harbour in a turbulent sea and strong wind when, at midday, the anchor hawser broke. The onshore wind caused the vessel to drift and between 5pm and 6pm had driven it onto a sandbank at Camber beach, which caused the *Georgiana* to sink extremely quickly. Her cargo of bricks, for the construction of the Battery at Dungeness, probably did not help the situation. Once the vessel was in serious difficulties the crew took to the rigging in an effort to save their lives.

The Camber station lifeboat, aware of the plight of the crew, spent two hours trying to launch their boat through the extensive surf and waves without success, at a cost of £6 to the National Lifeboat Institute. The problem was that the out-haul line used for launching had been removed for the summer period and therefore the crew had nothing to pull against to get through the boiling sea. As a result of not being able to effect a rescue the vessel sank with the loss of all hands.

At low tide the following day it was possible to walk to the wreck.

Emma & John (Aka James & Emma)

Date sunk:	2.6.1860
Location:	West of Rye harbour
Type:	London sailing barge
Cargo:	Timber
Home port:	London
Voyage:	London to Le Havre
Master:	Ainsworth
No. of passengers:	2
Ref:	LL No. 14404. 4.6.1860; HC 6.6.1860

This vessel was caught in the same turbulent seas and heavy wind that sunk the *Georgiana* (see page 115). The *Emma & John* was sailing eastward *en route* to Le Havre when the wind and sea drove the vessel ashore just west of Rye harbour.

The master had his wife and young daughter on board at the time. Unfortunately the girl was lost and drowned while trying to get her onto land, but luckily everyone else managed to get ashore safely.

Louise

Date sunk:	29.6.1861
Location:	8–10 miles (13–16km) south west of Hastings (Later salvaged)
Gross Tonnage:	120
Type:	French three-masted sailing schooner
Cargo:	Coal
Voyage:	Sunderland to Sables
Date built:	1861
Master:	Jaulin
No. of crew:	5
Ref:	SE 6.7.1861; HN 5.7.1861, 29.11.1861

On the morning of Saturday 29th June 1861 at about 10am there was a sudden squall accompanied by thunder and lightning. One vessel at sea at this time was the French schooner *Louise*, only three months old and on her maiden voyage. This vessel was 8–10 miles (13–16km) south west of Hastings with all her sails set when the squall suddenly struck with such ferocity that she capsized and sunk bow first before the crew even had time to take any of the sails down. The vessel finally came to rest on a sandbank in three fathoms of water. The master and two of his crew took to the rigging while the other three crew members got into the vessel's small boat. They had not gone far when this was capsized too because of the sea conditions. Fortunately the three men aboard managed to swim back to the wreck of the *Louise*.

About 2 miles (3km) away from the wreck was a brigantine from Guernsey called the *Rover,* which was sitting out the squall. Once the crew were aware of the plight of the *Louise* they launched their boat and managed to rescue the three crew members who swam back to the wreck. The remaining crew were picked up by a fishing smack that was also nearby and taken to Dover.

The demise of the vessel was witnessed by a number of coastguard stations, and boats from Bo Peep, Galley Hill, Bexhill, Kewhurst and Priory stations all put to sea to assist in the rescue. The boat from Bo Peep was under the command of the station's chief boatman Mr Gallaghar. Together with coastguards Dockings and French and two volunteers who happened to be by the station at the time (John Bray and Jeremiah Crittenden), he came alongside the boat from the *Rover*. The rescued crew were taken to the Hastings customs house. It was here that Mr Vizitelly, who was staying at Beach Cottages, acted as interpreter for the French crew. They were clothed and returned to the Dover Shipwrecked Seaman's Refuge free of charge by the South-Eastern Railway company.

Later Captain Gough, RN, the commander of the coastguard in the district, went out to the wreck in the Priory coastguard station galley and supervised the recovery of sails, stores and other items. The *Louise* was subsequently recovered and purchased by Mr C.T. How of St Leonards, who had it repaired and refitted by Messrs Kent of Hastings. It was launched after this re-fit on Saturday 23rd November 1861 opposite the Fishmarket at Hastings before a huge local crowd. The *Louise* was afloat again and bound for Wales on only her second voyage.

Willem Eduard

Date sunk:	1.12.1861
Location:	Ashore at Martello Tower No. 32, 3 miles (5km) west of Rye harbour
Type:	Dutch sailing schooner
Cargo:	Tobacco, hides, horsehair and general goods
Voyage:	Buenos Aires to London
Master:	M. Van Wyck
No. of crew:	8
Ref:	SIBI V2 section 3; SE 7.12.1861; FO 7.12.1861; HN 6.12.1861

By Saturday 30th November 1861 the *Willem Eduard* had been at sea for 87 days, having left Buenos Aires on 5th September bound for London. At 9.30pm the vessel was off Dungeness to the westward and apparently not displaying any lights. It was a very dark night with heavy seas and strong winds. Unbeknown to the crew, the HM steam sloop *Flying Fish* was bearing down on her *en route* to the west coast of Africa. The master of this ship was Commander Anderson. Suddenly the lookout on the *Flying Fish* saw the *Willem Eduard* through the terrible weather, but it was too late for the ship to alter course to avoid a collision. The *Flying Fish* struck the *Willem Eduard*, causing serious damage which resulted in the vessel rapidly taking in water. At the time of impact the mate on board the *Willem Eduard* had to jump onto the *Flying Fish* to save his life. He was later landed at Portsmouth when the *Flying Fish* put in there to have repair work done as a result of the collision.

As the *Willem Eduard* was so badly damaged and at great risk of sinking, the master, decided that in order to save his vessel, crew and the cargo he would run the vessel ashore. This he did near Martello Tower 32 early on Sunday morning. As a result of this action the crew were saved as was most of the cargo, although some was damaged. Unfortunately the vessel became a total wreck.

After the collision Commander Anderson searched the area for some hours to check for survivors and for the vessel itself, but without success. He was totally unaware that the *Willem Eduard* had run for the shore.

Daniel Wheeler

Date sunk:	6.3.1862
Location:	Ashore near Jury's Gap coastguard station
Cargo:	Ballast
Home port:	Scarborough
Voyage:	Le Havre to Newcastle
Ref:	SE 11.3.1862; HN 14.3.1862

On the night of Wednesday 6th March 1862 there was a severe storm blowing off Rye which caused this vessel to be driven ashore near Jury's Gap coastguard station. All the crew were safely rescued.

Thomas Snook

Date sunk:	30.6.1862
Location:	20 miles (32km) south of Hastings
Gross tonnage:	216
Type:	British brigantine
Voyage:	To Africa
Date built:	1834, London
Owner:	Forster & Co.
Master:	F. Woodward
No. of crew:	12
Ref:	SIBI V2 section 3; SE 5.7.1862; HC 2.7.1862

On the morning of Monday 30th June 1862, the *Thomas Snook* was bound for the African coast when it was in collision with the barque, *City of Carlisle,* a vessel of some 1,000 tons, bound for Bombay from London. The cause of this collision is not known but the *Thomas Snook* sank almost immediately as a result of the impact.

The vessel's master and two of his crew drowned as a result of the collision but the remainder of the crew were rescued by the *City of Carlisle*. The master of the *City of Carlisle* found that his vessel had sustained quite a bit of damage including a leak, so he hailed a steam tug and returned to London for the necessary repairs.

Clara

Date sunk:	29.11.1862
Location:	1 mile (1.6km) west of Haddocks coastguard station
Gross tonnage:	260
Type:	French brigantine
Cargo:	Grain
Home port:	Bordeaux
Voyage:	Grenville to Dunkirk
Master:	M. Esnol
No. of crew:	7
Ref:	LL No. 15179. 29.11.1862; HN 5.12.1862

Early in the morning of Saturday 29th November 1862, at low tide, this vessel was sailing up the English Channel in a strong south-easterly wind. It would appear that this was the reason that the vessel lost her course and struck the rocks beneath the cliffs east of Hastings, to the west of Haddocks coastguard station. Having struck the rocks the vessel heeled over and rapidly filled with water. The crew took to the boat and rowed to Hastings, landing opposite the fish market just after dawn.

As the *Clara* was a French vessel, the local French consul at Rye, Mr Vidler, was informed of the wreck, which the officer in charge of the coastguard in the district, Captain Gough, RN, took control of. Later in the day the vessel was inspected and found not to have sustained too much damage. As a result it was dismantled over that weekend and into Monday, but during Monday night a strong south-easterly wind blew up. The action of this wind and the sea soon broke up the hull until virtually nothing was left.

Benedictoire de Dieu

Date sunk:	12.5.1863
Location:	Ashore near Martello Tower No. 47
Type:	French *chasse-maree*
Cargo:	Nitrates and soda
Home port:	Boulogne
Voyage:	Le Havre to Dunkirk
Master:	Lemare
No. of crew:	3
No. of passengers:	2
Ref:	LL No. 15317. 14.5.1863; HN 15.5.1863; SE 16.5.1863; HC 20.5.1863

On the evening of Tuesday 12th May 1863 there was a storm raging with heavy rain. It was these conditions which caused this vessel, at about 11.45pm, to be driven ashore near to Martello Tower 47 at Bexhill and become a total wreck.

The Bexhill coastguard station, under the command of Mr J. Bulley, swung into action as soon as they were aware of this casualty. Mr Bulley summoned the life apparatus from the Bo Peep coastguard station, requesting that it be taken to where the vessel was ashore, because he feared the loss of the ship's crew. However, before this equipment arrived at the scene, Mr Bulley and three of his men managed to get aboard the stricken vessel and rescue the crew of three, a passenger and one boy, and get them back to shore. Approximately ten tons of the cargo was saved but the rest was washed away by the heavy seas.

The following day Mr Groom, the collector of customs, and Mr Vidler, the French consul from Rye, both visited the scene of the wreck.

Perseverance

Date sunk:	30.9.1863
Location:	Ashore at London Road, St Leonards
Type:	British sailing schooner
Cargo:	Coal
Owner:	Messrs Winter & Son
Ref:	SE 3.10.1863; HN 2.10.1863

On the afternoon of Wednesday 30th September 1863 a storm warning telegram was received at Hastings to 'hoist south-cone' as bad weather was expected. The telegram was well founded as during the evening a severe south-easterly storm broke with torrential rain which lasted into Thursday morning.

Onshore between St Leonards and Hastings were three vessels laden with coal. These were the *Perseverance* (at London Road, St Leonards), the *Milward* (at Bo Peep) and the *William Pitt* (at the fish market, Hastings). The storm was so severe that the *Perseverance* was dashed against an adjacent groyne which broke the vessel's back and one mast, causing it to become a total wreck. It had only recently been refitted.

Milward

Date sunk:	30.9.1863
Location:	Ashore at Bo Peep, St Leonards
Type:	Dandy
Cargo:	Coal
Home port:	Hastings
Owner:	Messrs Winter & Son
Ref:	SE 3.10.1863; HN 2.10.1863

This vessel had come ashore at Bo Peep, St Leonards to discharge its cargo of coal and, as mentioned on page 125, was one of three on shore at the time. A southerly storm had been forecast which duly arrived during the evening of 30th September 1863. Unfortunately it caused severe damage to the hull of the *Milward* by smashing the bulwarks, stoving a hole in the vessel's hull.

Thetis

Date sunk:	13.2.1864
Location:	Off Martello Tower No. 37, 6 miles (9.6km) south west of Rye.
Cargo:	Oysters
Home port:	Jersey
Voyage:	Dieppe to Newhaven
Owner:	John Carter
Master:	John Carter
No. of crew:	1
Ref:	SIBI V2 section 3; RNLI; SE 16.2.1864; HN 19.2.1864

A week before this incident happened, the *Thetis* had left Dieppe in the sole charge of its master. He sailed without his crew because they had all been drinking and did not want to go to sea. He was bound for Newhaven with his cargo of oysters and at 8.30am on Saturday 13th February 1864 was off Fairlight, which Carter assumed to be Beachy Head. Having made this error in the force five south-westerly storm that was blowing at the time, and being single-handed, it was not long before the vessel ran into difficulties and filled with water. In an effort to save himself Carter took to the rigging and hoped and prayed for rescue.

A coastguardman on duty at Martello Tower 36 was the first to see this vessel offshore in obvious difficulty with a man clinging to the rigging. The alarm was raised and the chief officer, Mr Buck, arranged for the lifeboat to be crewed, which included George Terry (42), and it set off for the *Thetis*. The payment of the crew and the cost to get the lifeboat launched with the use of three horses was £6.5s.

The lifeboat successfully came alongside the *Thetis* and managed to get Carter safely into the lifeboat. The lifeboat then set out to return and had nearly reached the shore when an exceptionally large wave hit it and knocked George Terry overboard. This wave also half-filled the lifeboat, making it impossible for it to manoeuvre to pick Terry up. The plan was to beach the lifeboat, empty it of water and return immediately to rescue him. However, the search for George Terry was fruitless. Mr Terry left a widow and six children, three or four of them being below the age to work. His body was found the following morning near Rye harbour.

On Monday 15th February an inquest was held at the Reading Room, Rye Harbour, to enquire into his death. After hearing the evidence, the coroner, Capt. R.C. Stileman, who was also the mayor of Winchelsea, recorded a verdict of accidental drowning.

This accident came to the knowledge of HRH the Prince of Wales and he gave a donation of £10.10s to the bereaved widow, in the form of a cheque sent to the local coastguard district commander.

Robin Hood

Date sunk:	21.11.1864
Location:	5 miles (8km) west of Dungeness
Gross tonnage:	800
Length (feet/metres):	204/62
Beam (feet/metres):	35/10
Type:	British sailing vessel
Cargo:	General goods
Home port:	Liverpool
Voyage:	London to Hong Kong
Date built:	1856, Aberdeen
Owner:	Beazley
Master:	J. Mann
No. of crew:	29
Ref:	LR. 1864-5.318(R); RNLI; HN 25.11.1864

During the night of Monday 21st November 1864, the *Robin Hood*, under the command of the master and his crew of 29 men, was sailing down the Channel when she was run down by a large ship running up. The name of this other vessel is unknown. The *Robin Hood* crew were soon into their boats and fortunately for them the steam tug *Conqueror*, from London, was nearby to pick up the majority. The remainder were picked up by other vessels in the area.

Two lifeboats from east and west of Rye harbour put to sea to assist in the rescue but only one of them managed to reach the vessel. When it arrived they found that the crew had already left. The cost of launching the lifeboat that did reach the vessel was £7.2s.6d. This included the cost of nine crew (10s per man), 13 helpers (2s per man), and four horses (5s per horse hired).

Reine des Patriachs

Date sunk:	15.8.1866
Location:	4 miles (6km) south east of Hastings
Type:	French smack
No. of crew:	8
Ref:	SIBI V2 section 3

This vessel became a wreck with the loss of two of the crew.

Henrick von Thorn

Date sunk:	15.11.1866
Location:	Ashore near Rye harbour
Gross tonnage:	250
Type:	Prussian sailing brigantine
Cargo:	Dried fruits, hemp, marble, pumice stones, bay leaves
Home port:	Stralsund
Voyage:	Leghorn to Antwerp
Owner:	C.A. Bug
Master:	J.H. Mayer
Ref:	LL No. 16411. 16.11.1866; SE 20.11.1866; HN 23.11.1866; HO 20.11.1866

At 10.30pm on the night of Thursday 15th November 1866 this vessel ran aground near Rye harbour, although the reason is unknown. However, the crew had to be rescued by the lifeboats from Winchelsea and Camber coastguard stations. The actions of the sea soon made the vessel a total loss. A few days later a number of divers, under the supervision of Mr Genn from Whitstable, tried to recover as much of the cargo as possible.

Lamburn

Date sunk:	18.11.1866
Location:	Ashore at Priory, Hastings
Gross tonnage:	80
Length (feet/metres):	62/19
Beam (feet/metres):	19/6
Type:	British sailing brigantine
Cargo:	Coal
Home port:	Hastings
Date built:	1833 Hastings
Owner:	Messrs Kent
Ref:	SIBI V2 section 3; HN 5.10.1849, 19.4.1867, 23.11.1866; HO 20.11.1866

This vessel was launched on 12th February 1833 at Hastings. On the evening of Saturday 17th November 1866, the *Lamburn* came ashore at the Priory, Hastings, opposite Alexandra and Albert Houses, Denmark Place, with its cargo of coal for a Mr Cloke of the Hastings Gas Company. The day had been fine and the cargo was discharged readily and without problems. The vessel had been left overnight broadside on. Unfortunately, during the night a southerly gale blew up and the vessel was very vulnerable to the impending bad weather.

The crew could see that the vessel was in some peril, with the wind and sea increasing on a rising tide. With only a small anchor out for the hauling-off rope, the position seemed hopeless. However, the crew remained on board until 4am attempting to save the vessel but by this time it had become too dangerous to stay any longer. The ferocity with which the heavy seas were striking the *Lamburn* had, by 6am, started to cause serious damage to the vessel. The vessel then started to roll after being suddenly struck by three particularly heavy waves in succession. She rolled over on her starboard side with the deck facing towards the sea. In this position, and with the constant battering of the sea, it was not long before the vessel started to break up and it soon became a total wreck.

Later that day, when the weather had calmed slightly, a group of men under the directions of the owners started to salvage what they could from the wreck. However, the weather was not yet finished with the *Lamburn* and it soon completed the work of the 'wreckers' for them. As the day progressed the wind turned north westerly and, with a heavy swell, caused the remainder of the hull to come almost upright, lifting the bows out of the water and ripping the remaining planking from the port side so that little remained.

The general opinion was that the *Lamburn* had probably not been very seaworthy due to its age. Apart from the financial loss to its owners, many were glad that the loss had been ashore and not at sea, where there may have been loss of life. The vessel had, in 1861, lain ashore for many months, so much so that local people had been complaining that the 'eyesore' was an obstruction of their sea view from the High Street. However, on Saturday 13th April that year, after much repairwork by the owners, the *Lamburn* was refloated only to meet its final demise five years later.

This was not the first maritime incident that the *Lamburn* had been involved in. On 28th September 1849, when off Hartlepool, she ran down another vessel, the *Elizabeth* of Whitby. When the collision occurred the master of the *Lamburn* was below, asleep, and the mate, who was in charge of the vessel at the time, was also below having gone to get something to eat and drink. Fortunately, the crew of the *Elizabeth* were all rescued by the *Lamburn* and taken into Hartlepool. The *Elizabeth* was insured for £800.

Startled Fawn

Date sunk:	19.12.1867
Location:	16 miles (25km) west of Dungeness and 10–12 miles (16–19km) off shore
Gross tonnage:	1160
Type:	British ship
Cargo:	Rice, seed, cotton, jute
Home port:	Liverpool
Voyage:	Calcutta to London
Owner:	G.H. Fletcher
Master:	King
No. of crew:	30
Ref:	LL No. 16752. 21.12.1867; HN 27.12.1867, 21.2.1868

The *Startled Fawn* had collected a pilot from the Isle of Wight and on the evening of Thursday 19th December 1867 was proceeding up the Channel. The master, a man aged about 60, had been confined to his cabin since the previous Thursday due to having had a paralytic fit.

There was a very thick fog at the time which was clearly the main cause of the subsequent collision between the *Startled Fawn* and the *Rushing Water*. The details of the latter vessel are detailed on page 136. It was at about 7.30pm in these atrocious conditions that the *Rushing Water* suddenly loomed into view not more than a ship's length away. It was far too late for either crew to avoid the collision as the *Startled Fawn* was doing about 6½ knots. The impact caused so much damage to the *Rushing Water* that it sank within seven minutes.

As soon as the vessels collided, the crew of the *Rushing Water* jumped aboard the *Startled Fawn,* except for the second mate, who had been knocked overboard by the impact. However, the *Startled Fawn* soon launched its boat and he was picked up quickly, only slightly injured.

Unfortunately, the *Startled Fawn* also sustained damage as a result of the collision. The combined crews, now numbering 44 in total, set about making sure the vessel stayed afloat by manning the pumps. Despite their efforts, the *Startled Fawn* was taking in water at an alarming rate and by midnight there was 15 feet (4.6m) of water in the first and second forward holds and she was slowly sinking by the bows. As the situation was now looking desperate, it was decided that all 44 men would take to the three boats of the *Startled Fawn*. The boats had been rowing for some considerable time when they came across the Hastings fishing lugger, *Little Polly* (Thomas White, master). The *Little Polly* took all the men on board and landed them at Hastings fish market at about 10am that morning.

Once ashore the crews were well looked after by the local people. Mr Stevenson and his daughter-in-law at the Rising Sun took in the masters, mates, pilot and 15 of the crew, and the remainder were taken care of by Mr Griffin at his eating house in George Street. The local agent for the Shipwrecked Mariners Society, Mr William Phillips, and the secretary Mr F.W. Staines, arranged for clothing for the crews and issued them with tickets to catch trains to wherever they wanted to go. The Society also paid for all their board and lodging while in the town.

Rushing Water

Date sunk:	19.12.1867
Location:	504515N 003750E; 16 miles (25km) west of Dungeness and 10-12 miles (16-19km) off shore in 15 fathoms of water; wreck No: 4436
Gross Tonnage:	422
Length (feet/metres):	128/39
Beam (feet/metres):	27/8
Type:	British sailing barque
Cargo:	Iron, coke, engine parts
Home port:	London
Voyage:	Sunderland to Madras
Date built, builder:	1864, Robinson at Sunderland
Owner:	Charles Newman
Master:	Pearson
No. of crew:	14
Ref:	LL No. 16752. 21.12.1867; LR. 1866-67. 490(R); HN 27.12.1867, 21.2.1868

See the *Startled Fawn* on page 134 for details.

John & James

Date sunk:	9.4.1868
Location:	Ashore at Bulverhythe, St Leonards
Tonnage:	10
Type:	Fishing boat
Home port:	Hastings
Owner:	Mrs Page, Bourne Street, Hastings
Ref:	HN 10.4.1868

It appears that this nearly new vessel was run ashore at Bulverhythe for some totally unexplained reason. At about 3am on the morning of Thursday 9th April 1868 this local fishing boat was seen to be on fire, which is assumed to have been started by the stove on board. Police Sergeant Raymond was the first person to notice the burning boat on the shore and he raised the alarm. The coastguard also attended the vessel. They found a man by the name of Harmer who lived in All Saints Street in the boat, much the worse for alcohol. All that Harmer said was that he could not give any explanation as to how the vessel caught fire. However, he did say that once the men had finally reached shore they had all gone for a drink in a nearby public house and that he had returned to the vessel afterwards and fell sleep. So it was never established whether the fire on the vessel started whilst at sea or after it was run ashore. The vessel, valued at £150, was a total wreck from the fire, with the oars and a few items from the deck being the only things being saved by the coastguard.

Fairy

Date sunk:	2.1.1869
Location:	Slipway at London Road, St Leonards
Gross tonnage:	90
Length (feet/metres):	71/21
Beam (feet/metres):	20/6
Type:	British schooner
Cargo:	Coal
Home port:	Hastings
Date built, builder:	1846, Friars Loose at Durham
Owner:	William Winter, Mr Eastland
Master:	Eastland
Ref:	HN 8.1.1869

This single-deck, two-masted schooner, when registered, was given the number 24402 and its Port of Rye registration number was 1.

On the afternoon of New Year's Day 1869, there was a severe storm which resulted in the *Fairy* and her cargo of coal being grounded at the slipway at London Road, St Leonards. There was another vessel at the fish market, the *Pelican*, and as the weather appeared to be getting worse it was decided at midnight to 'fleet' the vessels and take them to the moorings. Here they were made fast to await an improvement in the now quite turbulent weather. Of the two vessels, the *Fairy* was the least able to withstand the stresses and strains of the storm. After an hour a stanchion broke and the *Fairy* was driven ashore. The relentless beating of the waves soon washed the vessel across a groyne, which broke its back. The stern portion of the schooner remained more or less intact but most of the remaining two thirds of the vessel were ripped to pieces by the sea. The crew used the vessel's hawsers to get safely ashore.

The master had a half share in the vessel which was valued at about £200. His share had taken him many years to earn. As a result of this vessel becoming a wreck he had, in effect, lost his life's work in one storm. As stated elsewhere in this book, it was not possible to insure vessels that were beached to discharge their cargo.

The crew of the vessel lost all their clothing in the wreck and a local appeal was launched on their behalf to replace their belongings.

Pearl

Date sunk:	14.2.1869
Location:	Off Camber coastguard station
Type:	British sailing brig
Cargo:	200 tons of coal
Home port:	Shoreham
Voyage:	Newcastle upon Tyne to Shoreham
Owner:	Thomas Thwaites, Brighton
Master:	Robert Pierce
No. of crew:	8
Ref:	SIBI V2 section 3; RNLI; HN 19.2.1869

On Sunday 14th February 1869, soon after 10am, this vessel was *en route* to Shoreham, when off Bexhill she struck rocks and as a result sprang a leak. The master decided that he would change his course and run for Rye harbour. As the vessel approached Rye she had a great deal of water in the hold. With this and the wind now blowing a south-westerly gale, and the state of the tide, there was insufficient depth to allow the *Pearl* to run into the harbour. The vessel eventually went aground off the Camber coastguard station.

The *Pearl* was showing her distress signal which alerted the lifeboats at both Camber and Winchelsea, which were manned by the coastguard. The Winchelsea boat effected the rescue of the eight crew as it was the easier one of the two to launch. No sooner had the lifeboat got the stricken crew on board, than the sea threw the *Pearl* on her beam ends and she broke up.

Tyro

Date sunk:	3.6.1869
Location:	Off Hastings
Gross tonnage:	182
Length (feet/metres):	103/31
Beam (feet/metres):	23/7
Type:	British sailing brig
Home port:	Shoreham
Date built, builder:	1860, Lugworth, Grand River, Nova Scotia
Owner:	J. Billingshurst, Brighton
Master:	Richard Reeves
No. of crew:	8
Ref:	SIBI V2 section 3; HN 11.6.1869; HC 9.6.1869

At midday on Thursday 3rd June 1869, while the *Tyro* was under full sail on a starboard tack and approximately ten miles (16km) off Hastings, the *Mars,* weighing 1,700 tons was bearing down on her. The *Mars* was travelling eastward and attempted to miss the *Tyro* without altering course, by going astern of her. However, she struck the *Tyro* on the starboard side at or just aft of the main rigging. As soon as the collision had occurred both vessels turned into the wind and a boat was lowered from the *Mars* to pick up the *Tyro* crew. It was just as well this rescue was effected quickly as it took just 15 minutes for the *Tyro* to sink after impact.

This whole incident was witnessed by William Gallop the master of the *William and Mercy,* a Hastings fishing boat which was about 2 miles (3km) from them when the collision occurred. In Gallop's report of the incident to the chief officer of the coastguard, it was his opinion that the *Mars* was never going to clear the *Tyro* without a change of course. Gallop also told the coastguard that after the collision he made for the scene and when he arrived he called out to the *Mars* to ascertain if he could render assistance, but received no reply.

Mary Botwood

Date sunk:	8.9.1869
Location:	6 miles (9.6km) south east of Hastings
Type:	British schooner
Cargo:	Flint stone
Home port:	Aberystwyth
Voyage:	Dieppe to Runcorn
Date built:	1858, Cardiff
Ref:	SIBI V2 section 3

This vessel was lost after a collision in a force five north-westerly storm.

Belona

Date sunk: 1870
Location: Off Hastings
Type: Steamer
Ref: HO 5.3.1870

This is the vessel about which least is known regarding how she became a wreck. On Monday 28th February 1870, a bottle was washed ashore at the Camber coastguard station in which was found a note which read, 'Belona going down, all hands. Good bye'. Early on Wednesday morning parts of a wreck were washed ashore at Hastings. This seemed to have come from a large steamer which was assumed to have been the *Belona*.

Royal Albert

Date sunk:	6.6.1870
Location:	Off Hastings
Home port:	Hastings
Voyage:	Local pleasure trip
Date built:	1867
Master:	George Wenman
No. of crew:	1
No: of passengers:	16 approx.
Ref:	SIBI V2 section 3; HN 10.6.1870; HO 11.6.1870

This tragedy happened soon after 4pm on Whit Monday, 6th June 1870, with great loss of life. The ship's passengers were all trippers enjoying a short sail out to sea from Hastings beach. The incident happened on a fine day but with quite a strong easterly breeze.

The *Royal Albert* left the beach near the Albion Hotel, under the command of George Wenman. He was at the stern and Thomas Tichbon at the bow. On board were an unknown number of passengers, probably about 16. The vessel had been sailing for about ten minutes and was about half a mile from shore when a heavy gust of wind caught the sails. To counteract the effect of this gust, seven or eight of the passengers went to the windward side while the crew attempted to release the cleat holding the mainsheet. Their three attempts to release it were in vain as was the effect of the passengers to the windward side of the vessel. The gunwales went under the water causing the vessel to fill and sink, thus tipping all the occupants of the boat into the sea. Both crew members managed to swim safely to shore.

As soon as the vessel capsized a number of vessels from the beach put off to rescue the passengers. One such boat was Richard Gallop's rowing boat, which was already at sea taking a gentleman out for a trip. He was about 150 yards (137m) from the *Royal Albert* when he saw her capsize, and he immediately made for the scene. He rescued one of the *Royal Albert*'s passengers, a Mr John Chambers, who was visiting Hastings and staying at East Parade.

There were also a number of others who safely reached shore, namely Mr Archer, a jeweller of George Street, Hastings, Mr Thomas Paine of London and Ruth Winters, a young girl in the service of Mr H. Winter of George Street, Hastings. They were taken to the Cutter Inn and Rising Sun to recover.

One of the vessels that put off from the beach belonged to Richard Breeds, a fisherman of East Wall, Hastings, and he brought ashore two bodies of *Royal Albert* passengers, George Richards and Alfred Hayes. The bodies of two other passengers, Louisa Maynard and Fanny Chambers, were also soon found. A final total of nine people were to lose their lives as a result of this pleasure trip.

It was not long before a vast crowd had gathered on the beach to witness the events. The crowd grew so large that a considerable number of police, under the command of Superintendent Glenister, with the assistance of local fishermen, were required to form a barrier with the help of oars and spars to keep the crowd away from the rescuers.

The following afternoon, Tuesday 7th June, an inquest was held at Hastings town hall, before the coroner Mr F. Ticehurst, to identify the four bodies that were found, namely George Richards, Alfred Hayes, Louisa Maynard and Fanny Chambers. The inquest jury, consisting of tradesmen and residents from the High Street and George Street, viewed the bodies of the two women at the Cutter Inn, and those of the two men at Barton's warehouse.

Richards' father, Charles George Richards, gave evidence of identification to the Inquest. He told the inquest that his son was 27 years of age and had once been a clerk at the Bank of England, although he was at the time of his death unemployed. He said that his son had been staying in Hastings for about a month.

Hayes' body was identified by his brother, John Hayes of 88 St John's Street, Clerkenwell, London. He told the hearing that his brother was 25 years of age and that he had not seen him for about three or four weeks, as he had moved to Hastings to recuperate after an illness. The deceased had been lodging in the High Street with his wife and child for the previous three weeks.

Laura Blesymire, the sister of Louisa Maynard, gave evidence. She told the coroner and jury that her sister was a widow, 38 years of age, and she had last seen her sister alive at about 5pm on the previous Saturday, just before she left for Hastings. She also told the hearing that the deceased lived in Vale Place, Hammersmith, London.

Fanny Chambers' brother-in-law, James Chambers, a cabinet maker of 12 Regents Row, Queens Road, Dalston, gave evidence. He told the hearing that he was the brother of the deceased's husband, John, and that they lived at 1 Grange Street, Hoxton. He said that she was either 37 or 38 years of age and that her husband John was with her in the *Royal Albert* at the time. However, John was saved and taken to the Cutter Inn to recover.

Equator

Date sunk:	21.1.1871
Location:	10 miles (16km) off Hastings/6 miles (9.6km) off Bexhill, in 9 fathoms of water
Gross tonnage:	265
Length (feet/metres):	112/34
Beam (feet/metres):	24/7
Type:	British sailing brig
Cargo:	Molasses
Home port:	London
Voyage:	Cuba to Alloa
Date built, builder:	1869, Adamson at Grangemouth
Owner:	A. Adamson
Master:	William Lennox
No. of crew:	10
Ref:	SIBI V2 section 3; HN 27.1.1871, 3.2.1871, 10.2.1871, 31.3.1871; HO 28.1.1871

At about 6.10pm on Saturday 21st January 1871, the *Equator* was 9 miles (14km) off Hastings, under the command of the master, William Lennox, a seaman of some 20 years' experience. Although dark at the time, visibility was clear and there was a strong wind. The *Equator* was making good ground up the Channel with all her lights well trimmed, when the vessel's lookout called out to Lennox that there was a brig on the port bow. It was only then about 250ft (76m) away and not displaying any visible lights. Lennox was on deck at the time and as soon as he saw the vessel bearing down on them he called out, but received no response from the brig. There was little he could do as the brig was so close, and it struck the *Equator* on the port side within a few minutes of first being seen. As soon as the collision occurred, the *Equator* started rapidly to fill with water. Lennox gave orders to make ready the jolly boat, but before the crew could manage it the boat was floating clear of the vessel's decks. The crew got into the boat, with the master the last to leave. He was up to his shoulders in water when he finally left the sinking vessel which was in about nine fathoms of water. In fact he was just in time and had to take hold of one of the jolly boat's oars to actually get aboard.

One of the crew, James Barnes, a single man aged approximately 22, was at the helm when the collision occurred. Unfortunately he did not manage to get aboard the jolly boat. As the *Equator* started to go down, Barnes went to the stern of the vessel to get a lifebuoy, but the vessel sank before he could return to the jolly boat. The crew could hear his cries for help but they were powerless to help because the jolly boat did not have any usable oars. They were also worried about getting too close to their sinking vessel for fear that the suction would pull them down too.

Once the crew were safely in their jolly boat they called out to the brig that had run them down, but again there was no answer. The brig carried on its way. The crew drifted before the sea and wind and finally beached at about 8.30pm near Hastings pier at low tide. The crew called out for help, and fortunately the pier manager, Mr Dodson, and his staff heard their calls and waded into the sea up to their chests to bring the crew safely ashore. Once ashore Charles Marks, the chief officer of the Priory coastguard station, was made aware of the shipwrecked crew and Lennox related the story of their plight. Meanwhile the crew were taken care of by William Phillips, the local agent of the Shipwrecked Mariners Society, and were lodged at Griffin's eating house in Bourne Street, Hastings.

John Hicks, a coastguard boatman, had been made aware of the sinking of the *Equator* and that one of the crew was missing. As a result he kept a constant patrol on his part of the beach, and while on his patrols at about 7am on Monday 23rd January at low water, he found the body of the missing seaman James Barnes on the sand at Pett Level between Martello Towers 36 and 37. The lifebuoy was round his waist and his right hand was still holding it, while his left hand was in a swimming pose. However, the strange thing was that his hair was still dry. The body was taken to the White Hart Inn at Guestling until the inquest, which was held there the following Thursday. A carved arm from a figurehead and other wreckage that was washed ashore with Barnes' body was also taken to the White Hart.

The inquest on Thursday 26th January, was before the coroner Mr C. Shepherd, and a jury. One of the witnesses to give evidence was George Wenman, a pleasure boatman of 2 Coburg Place, Hastings, who told the court that he had taken Lennox and his mate home once they were ashore. These two told Wenman of their experience and blamed the collision on there being no lookout on the then unknown brig. Wenman said that Lennox had told him Barnes' home address was at Newton Abbot, Devon, and that he had written there and subsequently received a reply from Barnes' mother who was a nurse for the family at the address. Among other witnesses to give evidence was a surgeon, Mr L. Groome from Ore, Hastings, whose evidence was in relation to his examination of Barnes' body. He told the inquest that there were no signs or marks of violence on his body, or any fractured bones. He also said that there were no signs of drowning, based on the fact that the head hair was dry, and concluded that James Barnes had died from exposure and exhaustion. The coroner eventually decided, and the jury agreed, that the hearing should be adjourned because the local police superintendent, Mr Jeffery, had been unable to establish the name of the offending vessel and wanted more time to trace it.

The inquest was reconvened on Tuesday 31st January, again at the White Hart Inn, Guestling. One of the additional witnesses at this hearing was Lennox, who had returned from Scotland to give his evidence. He told the hearing of the circumstances as outlined above, and that he thought the cause of the collision was due to there being no lookout on the brig. He said that had there been such a lookout he would have seen the *Equator*. Charles Marks, the chief coastguard officer at the Priory coastguard station, told the inquest that the *Equator* was on a proper course according to Admiralty regulations. However, at the end of the hearing the coroner told the jury that after having heard all the available evidence, they had not heard from anybody from the offending vessel, which would make it difficult for them to reach a verdict of manslaughter, or to decide whether the collision was due to neglect, despite enquiries made by Superintendent Jeffery. As a result of this direction the jury agreed a verdict: Barnes had died from exposure and exhaustion and was washed ashore after the *Equator* was in collision with an unknown vessel.

Using the recovered wreckage to trace the offending vessel, enquiries by Charles Marks, the chief coastguard officer, finally took him to Ramsgate where a Greek brig *Artemis*, had put in for repairs. The vessel was in ballast *en route* from Le Havre to Cardiff. When Marks went to Ramsgate with the missing arm of the figurehead, he was greeted with much enthusiasm by the crew which confirmed his suspicions that it had come from this vessel. As a result of his enquiries, an Admiralty court hearing was held before Sir R. Phillimore on 23rd and 24th March 1871.

The master and mate of the *Artemis* denied they were responsible for the collision with the *Equator*, but Sir Phillimore in his judgement to the court said: 'We are of the opinion that the *Equator* was close-hauled on the starboard tack, and therefore it was the duty of the *Artemis* to keep out of the way, which she neglected to do. I therefore pronounce the *Artemis* alone to blame.'

As the *Equator* was only two years old when this collision happened, it had been insured for a large sum of money with three marine insurance companies. The Admiralty court judgement ensured that the underwriters did not withstand the loss.

T.W.Webb

Date sunk:	20.5.1871
Location:	Off Dungeness
Type:	Iron screw steamer
Cargo:	640 tons of rails
Home port:	Hartlepool
Voyage:	Middlesbrough to Taganrog
Owner:	Messrs Wilkinson, Watt & Co.
Master:	Green
No. of crew:	20
Ref:	LL No. 17814. 23.5.1871; SE 27.5.1871; HN 26.5.1871; HO 27.5.1871; HC 24.5.1871

At about 9.30pm on Saturday 20th May 1871, the *T.W. Webb*, under the command of the master and his crew of 20 men, was off Dungeness in good weather and bound for the Baltic, when a ship's light was seen ahead. Green took the necessary evasive course to give the oncoming vessel a wide berth. However, when both vessels were about 800 yards (731m) apart, the oncoming vessel, which transpired to be the steamer *Paraquay* of Waterford, suddenly changed course and came straight for the *T.W. Webb*.

Green again saw the impending danger to his vessel and ordered his engines full speed astern, but to little effect as within a few minutes the *Paraquay* struck the *T.W. Webb* on the starboard bow, causing severe damage to and below the water line. This damage was so severe that she sank within two minutes of the impact. At the time of the impact, Green and four of his crew named Jakes, Bargewell, Green and Foster, managed to jump from the fore rigging of the *T.W. Webb* onto the chains of the *Paraquay* and reach her decks safely. Two other crew members, Mowatt and Coulson, tried to follow, intending also to go up the chains of the *Paraquay*, but they unfortunately fell overboard in the attempt. A boat was got ready from the *Paraquay* and after several minutes managed to rescue these two crewmen from the sea, who by then were quite exhausted.

The master and the six crew members were the only ones saved. The 14 remaining crew consisting of Hector Williams (mate), J. Payne (second mate), Hadey (cook), Morfee (carpenter), Gray (chief engineer), Watson (second engineer), Garland (third engineer), Dixon (fireman), Giles (fireman), Macartney (fireman), Parson (seaman), and three other seamen whose names are not known, were all lost. Morfee was from Rye and left a wife and six children. The remainder of the crew were also family men and lived in West Hartlepool.

As a result of this collision, the *Paraquay* also sustained much damage and set off to the Victoria docks, London, for repair work. However, *en route* the rescued crew from the *T.W. Webb* were put ashore at Gravesend, Kent.

Agnes Campbell

Date sunk: 17.11.1871
Location: 8 miles (13km) south of Galley Hill, Bexhill, in 8½ fathoms
Type: Schooner
Ref: HA 23.11.1871

Pilot Cutter No. 12

Date sunk:	16.2.1871
Location:	9 miles (14km) off Ecclesbourne.
Gross Tonnage:	75
Type:	Belgian iron pilot cutter
No. of crew:	6
Ref:	HG 24.2.1872; HN 23.2.1872

Early in the morning of Friday 16th February 1871, this cutter was off Ecclesbourne in thick mist and fog, when a barque suddenly came out of the fog and collided with it. The barque did not stop. The crew of the cutter soon realised that their vessel was badly damaged and got their jolly boat ready in order to abandon the ship. Fortunately for the crew, a local fishing boat, RX54, was nearby and the crew made for it. The fishing boat later landed them at Hastings. It took just 20 to 30 minutes for the cutter to sink without trace.

The master had been with the Belgian government pilot service for 20 years but this was his first voyage in command. It transpired that he had put his last pilot on board another vessel at about 6pm the night before, when off Beachy Head.

Hermes

Date sunk:	5.12.1872
Location:	2 miles (3km) east of Rye
Type:	Norwegian sailing brig
Cargo:	Rye
Home port:	Stavanger
Voyage:	Rouen to Stavanger
Owner:	S.A. Kohler
Master:	Astrup
No. of crew:	7 and 1 boy
Ref:	SIBI V2 section 3; RNLI; SE 10.12.1872

At 3am on Thursday 5th December 1872, this vessel was driven ashore in a force ten south-westerly gale. It was decided that one of the crew, who was wearing a lifebelt, together with the ship's boy, would take to the jolly boat to get help for the rest of the crew. The sea conditions were such that the jolly boat soon capsized with the loss of the ship's boy. However, the 25-year-old surviving crewman made it to the shore and was taken to the Crown Inn, Rye, whose licensee was Isaac Wright. The Norwegian vice-consul was informed of the tragedy and he attended the scene and took care of the survivor.

It transpired that this crewman was to be the only survivor because the remaining crew perished before help could reach them. The *Hermes* was eventually smashed to pieces by the combined effects of the rough seas and gale force winds.

A local lifeboat, the *Arthur Fitzroy*, was put off to assist in a rescue attempt but by the time it was launched and reached the *Hermes*, it was already a total wreck. It took 13 crew (each paid £1), 13 helpers (each paid 3s) and six horses to get the lifeboat launched at a total cost of £16.2s.6d.

Vesuvius

Date sunk:	7.4.1876
Location:	3 miles (5km) south of Hastings
Gross tonnage:	2,300
Type:	Dutch steamship
Cargo:	2,210 tons of wheat, wine, raisins
Voyage:	Odessa to Amsterdam
Owner:	Royal Netherlands Steam Navigation Company
Master:	Daarnhouwer
No. of crew:	32
Ref:	LL No. 19332. 8.4.1876; HN 14.4.1876, 28.7.1876, 4.8.1876, 25.8.1876

This large Dutch merchant ship was originally an English vessel called the *Avon*, from Sunderland.

At about 7am on Wednesday 5th July 1876 in fine weather and with three-mile visibility, the *Vesuvius* was steaming up the channel at about six knots. The steamship that she was to collide with, the *Savernake*, was steaming at about seven to eight knots, in the opposite direction. The *Savernake*, of 394 tons, was *en route* to Plymouth from Sunderland with its cargo of coal, under the command of the master, Walker, and his 16 crew.

The vessels were, in effect, on a head-on course but neither could see the other because the smoke from the *Savernake* was obliterating the view ahead for both ships. The first the crew of the *Vesuvius* actually saw of the *Savernake* was when they were about a ship's length apart, whereas the crew of the *Savernake* did not see the *Vesuvius* until they were about 200 yards (183m) apart. The masters of both vessels took all the evasive action they could to avoid the collision but to no avail, and the *Vesuvius* struck the stern of the *Savernake* with her starboard side.

The vessels collided with such force that the *Vesuvius* went down within 30 minutes of the impact. This was fortunately sufficient time for most of the crew to get into the jolly boats although with only ten minutes to spare before the ship went down. Two of the crew jumped onto the *Savernake* at the time of the collision and one crew member fell overboard, but was later picked up by a jolly boat put off from the *Savernake*.

The *Savernake* did not escape damage. In fact, to prevent her from sinking too, the master ran for Hastings beach. At the time of the collision there were a couple of Hastings fishermen, 'Groko' Kent and Mark Martin, nearby and it was they that led the *Savernake* to the beach and to safety at Hastings fish market.

There was no loss of life as a result of these two ships colliding, but two of the *Vesuvius* crew were injured, namely W. Saeyers and H. Phillips. Luckily, their injuries were not severe being mainly shock, and they were treated at the Hastings infirmary by Mr Penhall.

During the early part of August 1876 at the Admiralty court, the Right Hon. Sir R.J. Phillimore, heard evidence from representatives of both ships as to the cause of the collision. Mr Butt QC, Mr Clarkson and Mr Hannen appeared on behalf of the owners of the *Vesuvius*, whereas those appearing on behalf of the owners of the *Savernake* were Mr Milward QC, Mr Myburgh and Mr Lamb. At the end of the hearing the court decreed that both vessels were equally to blame for the collision.

Due to the size of the wreck it was decided by the Trinity Board that it would have to be blown up. It was at the time thought to be the biggest wreck to be blown up. The Trinity boat, the *Irene*, under the command of Captain Hatherley, was dispatched to deal with the wreck. Also on board this ship was Admiral Sir Richard Collinson who had come to assist and supervise, and the Trinity Board diver Mr Tatham, whose job was to lay the charges that would blow the wreck up. The *Irene* was stationed about 200 yards (183m) from the wreck for about a week while this operation was carried out.

The charges that were laid by Mr Tatham consisted of gunpowder and cotton powder packed into rubber bags which were then hermetically sealed. This was sufficient to keep the powders dry under 30 feet (9m) of water. From the mouth of each bag was a wire which trailed back to a magneto-dynamic exploder (the firing mechanism) on the *Irene*, under the control of a Professor Able who actually fired the charges. Some of these charges had up to 500lbs (226kg) of gun powder in them which, when fired, caused a plume of water to rise 50 feet (15m) above the sea. Each explosion killed a large amount of fish (several hundredweight), which were gleefully collected by the local fishermen. Eventually the wreck was destroyed but not until some 2000lbs (907kg) of gun-powder and 600lbs (272kg) of cotton powder had been expended on its destruction.

Clio

Date sunk:	5.7.1876
Location:	6 miles (9.6km) south east of Royal Sovereign Light
Length (feet/metres):	111/34
Beam (feet/metres):	27/8
Type:	British sailing barque
Cargo:	Iron, cattle fodder
Home port:	London
Voyage:	Cabes to Newcastle upon Tyne
Date built:	1845, Sunderland
Owner:	Harrison, Whitby
Master:	F. Leng
No. of crew:	10
Ref:	SIBI V2 section 3

This vessel collided with the steamship *Marentha* in a force four south-westerly wind.

Elsie Linck

Date sunk:	10.11.1876
Location:	1 mile (1.6km) south of Royal Sovereign Light in 15 fathoms
Type:	German sailing barque
Home port:	Danzig
Voyage:	London to Deboy
Date built:	1866
Master:	W. Pupp
No. of crew:	14
Ref:	SIBI V2 section 3; HN 21.11.1876; EG 15.11.1876, 11.4.1888; EC 18.11.1876

At about 11am on Friday 10th November 1876 with the weather fine, fishermen on the beach at Eastbourne heard the warning guns fired from the Royal Sovereign Light. On hearing this, two luggers from Eastbourne beach, one belonging to Mr G. Hyde, the other belonging to Mr Gausden, put off to see if they could assist with whatever the problem was. En route to the Royal Sovereign Light the two luggers came across the *Ben Lomond,* a steam tug, under the command of Mr M.J. Hardy, who accompanied the two luggers on their search. They were about ¼ mile (400m) south of the Royal Sovereign Light when they found the *Elsie Linck* which was slowly sinking bow first, in about 15 fathoms of water. The crew of the tug boarded the *Elsie Linck* but found the crew had already left. It was later found that the vessel had just collided with the German mail steam packet the *Euphrates*, who had taken the crew from the stricken vessel on board. The crew were later landed at Flushing.

The *Ben Lomond* put a line on the sinking vessel with the intention of salvaging her by towing her to shore. However, this was unsuccessful. By the time the tow was attempted the bow of the vessel was on the seabed preventing the tug moving her, and so the tow was abandoned. When the tug returned to Eastbourne, Mr Hardy, the master submitted a report to the local Lloyd's sub-agent

Mr T. Bennett covering the above circumstances. For some days after this event, 20 feet (6m) of the stern of the *Elsie Linck* was still visible at low water.

Charlotte

Date sunk:	3.8.1877
Location:	Fairlight coastguard station
Type:	British sailing lugger
Cargo:	Stone
Home port:	Rye
Voyage:	Rye to unknown destination
Owner:	J. Morris
Master:	J. Morris
No. of crew:	2
Ref:	SIBI V2 section 3

This vessel sank while being loaded with stone in a force five south-westerly wind.

Victory

Date sunk:	3.8.1877
Location:	Ashore at Fairlight coastguard station
Cargo:	Stone
Home port:	Rye
Owner:	Mrs Hoad, Rye
Master:	J. Morris
No. of crew:	3
Ref:	SIBI V2 section 3

This vessel was driven ashore in a force five south-westerly wind.

Prince Imperial

Date sunk:	8.9.1877
Location:	Ashore opposite 100, Marina, St Leonards
Type:	British fishing smack (originally French)
Home port:	Dover
Owner:	Henry Hammon
Master:	Henry Hammon
No. of crew:	3
Ref:	SIBI V2 section 3; HO 15.9.1877; HC 12.9.1877

This was originally a French fishing boat and had only recently been bought by the current owners.

At about 5am on Saturday 8th September 1877, this fishing boat was at anchor in Rye Bay in a strong southeasterly wind and rough seas. Suddenly the anchor chain broke and, it is not known if it was this or a coincidence, the vessel then sprang a leak. This was so serious that it was obvious the boat was in dire straits and likely to sink.

The master decided to run for Newhaven and he, together with the crew, constantly used buckets to bail out the water from the boat. However, their attempts to stem the rising water level were not effective and so Hammon decided that the best thing was to make a run for the shore to save both boat and crew. He beached the *Prince Imperial* at Marina, St Leonards, where he was met by the chief officer from the Priory coastguard station, Mr Reed, and a number of his men. With their assistance a hawser, which was fixed to the bow of the vessel, was secured to one of the groynes. Unfortunately the rough sea drifted the boat nearer and nearer the sea wall and by 11.30am she was in a very precarious state. The bow burst open allowing the sea to rush in, swamping the boat completely, and, with the action of the sea smashing it against the sea wall, it soon became a total wreck.

The crew got off safely and were assisted by Mr Moulton, the local secretary of the Shipwrecked Mariner's Society, to return to their homes free of charge.

It appears that the *Prince Imperial* was a very old boat. However, in the afternoon Mr Corps from St Leonards bought the wreck for £5.

Zeal

Date sunk:	4.11.1877
Location:	6 miles (9.6km) south east of Hastings
Type:	British fishing smack
Home port:	Rye
Date built:	1873
Owner:	Hoad Brothers, Rye
Master:	W.J. Foord
No. of crew:	4
Ref:	SIBI V2 section 3; HT 10.11.1877; HN 9.11.1877

In good visibility and with a light southerly breeze blowing, this local fishing smack was off Winchelsea at 3am on Sunday 4th November 1877 when she was run down by the steamship *Samuel Howard*. This ship struck the fishing smack amidships, and the damage was so severe that the *Zeal* sank within a couple of minutes. However, the crew managed to get into their jolly boat before the vessel went down. The *Samuel Howard* stopped, picked up the stranded crew and brought them close to Hastings, where the crew got back into their jolly boat and rowed ashore.

The circumstances of this incident were reported to Mr Smith, the chief officer at Hastings coastguard station. It appears that the *Zeal* was not at fault as the vessel was showing a bright light at the time. Having given all the details to Mr Smith, the crew returned to Rye on the train.

Donna Maria

Date sunk:	25.11.1877
Location:	Beachy Head bearing west by north, Fairlight Church north north-east; 6 miles (9.6km) off (Lovers' Seat), Hastings in 9 fathoms of water
Gross tonnage:	800
Length (feet/metres):	162/49
Beam (feet/metres):	32/9
Type:	British sailing barque
Cargo:	Coal
Home port:	South Shields
Voyage:	South Shields to Savana
Date built, builder:	1861, P. Valin, Quebec, Canada
Owner:	T.F. Tully
Master:	Andrew Whyte
No. of crew:	16
Ref:	LR. 1877–78. 363(D); LL No. 19841. 27.11.1877; HN 30.11.1877, 7.12.1877; HA 29.11.1877, 6.12.1877; HT 1.12.1877

At 11pm on Monday 24th November 1877 the crew saw a light which they took to be the Cape Gris Nez Light, and suddenly struck rocks which caused a leak in the vessel's hull. The pumps were manned by the crew but unfortunately the water entering the vessel was greater than the pumps could manage. After a night of pumping it became apparent that they were not going to save the *Donna Maria* and the decision was made to get the longboat ready and abandon the vessel. At 11am the crew finally left the *Donna Maria* with the sea breaking over the vessel's decks and the ship obviously about to sink at any moment. As a result the crew took to their longboat and were soon picked up by the steam tug *Express* and taken safely to Newhaven.

The Ecclesbourne and Fairlight coastguard station lookouts were totally unaware of what had happened. The first they knew of anything untoward was at 3pm when the grey skies and poor visibility cleared a little and they could see three masts sticking out of the sea. Fearing the worst, a coastguard boat was put off to investigate but as the evening was drawing in they were unable to locate the three masts. The following morning at daybreak another coastguard boat was put off under the command of Mr Smith, chief officer of Hastings coastguard and the chief officer from Ecclesbourne, and it was they that found the wreck *'on the bank'* off Lovers' Seat lying in nine fathoms of water. Finding nobody, the coastguard feared that the entire crew had perished. It was not until two or three hours later that they received a telegram from Newhaven informing them that the crew were all safe.

As the three masts of the *Donna Maria* were clearly a hazard to other shipping, on Tuesday 4th December 1877 the Trinity Board steamer *Galatea* arrived at the scene of the wreck and removed the three masts. It was decided that the hull would be left as there was sufficient water above her not to impede shipping.

Fanny

Date sunk: 9.12.1877
Location: 12 miles (19km) south of Hastings
Type: British sailing schooner
Ref: SIBI V2 section 3

This vessel sank after a collision with brig, *Senhora*.

Vier Broeders

Date sunk:	18.12.1877
Location:	Off Winchelsea coastguard station
Type:	Dutch sailing galliot
Cargo:	Potatoes
Home Port:	Gronigen
Voyage:	Gronigen to Portsmouth
Date built:	1862
Owner:	J.G. Berg, Sappemeer, Holland
Master:	Blok
No. of crew:	4
Ref:	SIBI V2 section 3; HN 28.12.1877; SE 25.12.1877

At about 6.45pm on Saturday 18th December 1877 this vessel ran into a storm while off Winchelsea. The sea was exceptionally rough and the driving rain made conditions very unpleasant for the crew. The conditions eventually drove the vessel aground to the west of Rye harbour and it was not long before she was swamped and sunk in about two fathoms of water. The crew climbed into the vessel's rigging to save themselves from the rough seas that were breaking over her.

The Winchelsea lifeboat of the National Lifeboat Institute was aware of this vessel's plight and launched their boat to assist the crew. It took two hours of rowing before the lifeboat actually got to the *Vier Broeders* and was then able to rescue the crew from the rigging. The lifeboat returned to Winchelsea at about midnight with the rescued crew.

London Packet

Date sunk:	7.3.1878
Location:	3 miles (5km) north east of Royal Sovereign Light
Gross tonnage:	69
Length (feet/metres):	58/17
Beam (feet/metres):	17/5
Type:	British sailing schooner
Cargo:	Oil; 98 tons of wheat
Home port:	Ipswich
Voyage:	London to Plymouth
Date built, builder:	1840, Bayley at Ipswich
Owner:	T. Whalebone
Master:	T. Whalebone
No. of crew:	3 and 1 boy
Ref:	SIBI V2 section 3; HC 13.3.1878; FE 16.3.1878; HO 9.3.1878; HI 12.3.1878

The *London Packet* left London on 26th February 1878, bound for Plymouth with her cargo of wheat. By 5th March she was off the Sussex coast in very strong westerly winds, reaching force seven. Due to the conditions she was unable to make any progress much beyond Brighton, and spent the next three days between there and Hastings. It was while in this situation at about 8.30pm on Thursday 7th March that the ship's boy had occasion to go below only to find that the vessel was shipping water very rapidly. The last time anybody had been below was at about 4pm for the four-hourly testing of the pumps. At this time there was no sign of any leak in the vessel.

The speed at which the *London Packet* was filling with water meant that if nothing was done soon, the vessel would quickly sink. It was apparent that the ship's pumps would not be able to keep pace with the level of water entering the vessel, so the master decided that he would run for shore as quickly as possible. In the meantime, the crew got the jolly boat ready, launched it and loaded their belongings. At 10.30pm the water was coming over the vessel's rails and it was at this point that the decision was made to leave the *London Packet*. The crew manned the oars of the jolly boat and pulled away.

The *London Packet* was carrying a quantity of oil and the action of the waves caused this to spill out over the sea around the vessel. This was somewhat fortunate for the crew as it had the effect of calming the sea's surface. The *London Packet* eventually sank in about five fathoms of water. Once the cargo of wheat came into contact with the water, it started to swell and this eventually forced out the sides of the vessel. This, coupled with the action of the sea, broke the vessel up into many pieces. It was insured for £300.

Fortunately for the crew, the master knew this part of the coast very well and decided to make for Hastings pier. It was just as well that they did, because the sea was such that had they attempted to land anywhere else their boat would have been smashed to pieces. It took the crew nearly three hours of great effort to arrive at Hastings pier at 1.15am the following morning. They were met by the local coastguard and taken to the Priory coastguard station where they stayed until midday the following day, when Mr Moulton, secretary of the Shipwrecked Mariners Society, gave them money and travel passes to return home.

The vessel's master sold the jolly boat they had used for £1 to a local fisherman.

Cyrus

Date sunk:	15.3.1878
Location:	Rye Bay
Gross tonnage:	68
Length (feet/metres):	62/19
Beam (feet/metres):	17/5
Type:	British sailing schooner
Cargo:	30 tons of ballast
Home port:	Rye
Voyage:	Hastings to Rye
Date built:	1819, Great Yarmouth
Owner:	James Collins Hoad, Robert Jones Hoad, Lewis Hoad
Master:	J. Holland
No. of crew:	4
Ref:	SIBI V2 section 3

This vessel's official number was 6514 and its Port of Rye registration number was 2. It had one deck and two masts. It sank with the loss of all the crew in a force six south-westerly gale with a cargo of 30 tons of ballast. The part-owner James Collins Hoad's business address was 20 Watchbell Street, Rye.

Commerce

Date sunk:	26.9.1878
Location:	6 miles (9.6km) off Fairlight, south east of Hastings
Gross tonnage:	1297
Length (feet/metres):	190/58
Beam (feet/metres):	38/11
Type:	Canadian sailing vessel
Cargo:	2,000 tons of wheat
Home port:	Shelbourne, Nova Scotia
Voyage:	Philadelphia to Antwerp
Date built, builder:	1877, John Bower & Freeman Pentz at Shelbourne, Nova Scotia
Owner:	L. Willett, J. Bower, E. Murphy
Master:	Elijah Nickerson
No. of crew:	17 and 1 boy
Ref:	SIBI V2 section 3; HO 28.9.1878, 18.1.1879; HN 27.9.1878, 11.10.1878

The *Commerce* had left Philadelphia with its cargo of 2,000 tons of wheat, 30 days prior to the accident. The other vessel involved, the *Empusa*, was a steamship collier of 2,000 tons in ballast, *en route* for Cardiff from London to collect a cargo of coal.

At about 4am on Thursday 26th September 1878, when 6 miles off Fairlight, south east of Hastings, these two vessels were approaching each other in clear weather and with a slight breeze blowing. Suddenly, and without warning, the *Empusa* altered its course and ran into the port side of the *Commerce*. This made a large hole in the *Commerce* which caused her to sink within ten minutes of the impact. The reason for the sudden change of course was because the mate, who was the officer on watch aboard the *Empusa*, thought the *Commerce* was a fishing boat and was trying to miss her fishing nets. It was not until he got closer to the *Commerce* that he realised this was not the case, and by then it was too late and the vessels collided, despite the *Commerce* displaying the necessary lights.

Sixteen of the crew from the *Commerce* managed to climb onto the *Empusa* and were saved. However, one of the crew (the forward lookout) and the cabin boy, aged 13, were drowned, pulled under by the suction effect when the *Commerce* sank. The boy, an orphan, had been taken under the 'wing' of Nickerson, the master of the *Commerce*, who had treated him like a son. When the collision happened, the boy climbed up the rigging of the *Commerce* and was clinging onto it calling out for Nickerson. However, despite a number of attempts by the crew to rescue him, he was too frightened to let go of the rigging and so went down with the vessel.

The rescued crew members, mostly Americans, were taken by the slightly damaged *Empusa* to within about 2 miles (3km) of the shore at Hastings, where she dropped anchor nearly five hours after the collision. They then got to the shore in a boat that had been saved from the *Commerce*. Mr Nickerson lost a watch that he had been presented with for services rendered to the United States of America. Later that same evening the crew were sent to a sailor's home in London by Mr Moulton, secretary of the local Shipwrecked Mariners Society.

At a subsequent Board of Trade inquiry held at Cardiff on 8th October 1878, before Mr R.O. Jones, Admiral Powell and Captain Castle, evidence was given by the two crews, which differed regarding the events of the collision. Those on the stricken *Commerce* stated that their vessel's lights were burning and that the *Empusa's* change of course just prior to the collision was the cause. The master of the *Empusa* said that he was in the chart room at the time, having left the ship under the control of his mate, because he had his wife and daughter on board with him. He said that as soon as the collision had happened, the mate lowered the starboard boat at once, although the rescued crew had climbed up ropes from the *Empusa*. The *Commerce* crew disputed this saying it was their own master who had ordered the lowering of the starboard boat once on board the *Empusa,* to save his crew. The mate on the *Empusa* said he did not see any lights on the *Commerce*, but did see a vessel which he had been watching for several minutes, assuming it to be a fishing boat. This was why he had altered course to starboard to avoid what he thought were fishing nets. He said that having realised the true situation he had ordered the engine full speed astern. However, the engineer in the engine room stated that he had never received any such order from the mate.

The court heard all the evidence and found the mate guilty of leaving the bridge having seen a light and not having ascertained what that light was. He had also left the bridge with only a boy in charge of the helm who was totally inexperienced and not competent to helm the vessel alone. They also found him guilty of running the vessel at high speed through what was a very busy stretch of sea. As a result they suspended his mate's certificate for six months.

On 11th January 1879, the owners of the *Empusa* brought an action in the Admiralty Court before Sir R.J. Phillimore, to limit their liability to the owners of the *Commerce*. Mr Webster QC and Mr Myburgh represented the owners of the *Empusa*, and Mr Milward QC and Mr Clarkson the owners of the *Commerce*. Mr Stubbs represented the owners of the cargo of wheat the *Commerce* had been carrying. The owners of the *Empusa*, having admitted negligence, were now asking the court only to be liable to pay £8,805, which represented £8 per ton of the gross tonnage of the *Empusa*. The owners of the *Commerce* argued that the gross tonnage was not as alleged and that the Empusa, not having an efficient crew, caused the collision. They also alleged that one of the owners was the master of the vessel who was in fact on board at the time of the collision. The court ordered that there would be a limitation of liability for the owners of the *Empusa*, in that they had to pay into court monies in respect of life claims and that they undertook to pay any further monies that the court may order. The owners of the *Commerce* were 'condemned' because of the extra costs incurred caused by them raising a number of other issues.

Ebenezer

Date sunk:	10.11.1878
Location:	9 miles (14km) south east of Fairlight coastguard station
Type:	German sailing barque
Cargo:	General goods
Home port:	Danzic
Voyage:	Le Havre to Buenos Aires
Date built:	1866
Owner:	J. Hoeniman, Danzic
Master:	C.A.B. Apreck
No. of crew:	10
Ref:	SIBI V2 section 3; HC 20.11.1878

On the night of Sunday 10th November 1878 there was a terrific force ten south-westerly gale off the East Sussex coast, and among the vessels at sea that night were the *Ebenezer* and the *Ferndale*.

It was the *Ebenezer* that suffered at the hands of the storm and exceptionally heavy seas, so much so that the crew decided to abandon the vessel. Distress flares were fired to attract attention to their plight and fortunately for the crew the nearby *Ferndale* saw the flares. The *Ferndale* made towards the flares and when they arrived they found that the *Ebenezer* was in imminent danger of sinking. The master launched his boats to rescue the crew and this was successful. All the crew were safely rescued. This in itself was no mean feat, bearing in mind the terrible conditions at the time.

The Trinity House steamer *Galatea* later visited the scene of the sinking and had the masts of the *Ebenezer* removed so as not to be a hazard to shipping.

Allison

Date sunk:	14.1.1879
Location:	East of Rye harbour
Gross tonnage:	212
Length (feet/metres):	86/26
Beam (feet/metres):	24/7
Type:	British sailing brig
Home port:	Whitby
Voyage:	Trouville to Newcastle upon Tyne
Date built:	1838, Sunderland
Owner:	T. Mennell
Master:	D. Clark
No. of crew:	7
Ref:	SIBI V2 section 3; RNLI; HC 22.1.1879; SE 18.1.1879

The *Allison* was off Rye harbour at anchor sitting out a force six south-westerly gale when the vessel's stern post (which the anchor cable was attached to) broke. The vessel was then adrift in the gale and inevitably was driven ashore.

Fortunately, the Camber coastguard had seen the vessel's predicament and had launched their lifeboat. They successfully managed to rescue the entire crew. However, it was an expensive lifeboat launch, not only in monetary terms but also in terms of manpower. The 13 men of the lifeboat crew were each paid 10s.d. There were 14 helpers, each paid 3s.6d. and a further five helpers who were each paid 1s. They helped launch and recover the lifeboat, together with the four horses, at a cost of 7s each, and their two drivers were each paid 2s. Apart from the lifeboat crew, the most highly paid person involved was the messenger who went for the horses. He was paid 7s for his work.

Appollo

Date sunk:	18.2.1879
Location:	Ashore east of Rock-a-Nore, Hastings
Gross tonnage:	98
Type:	Danish sailing schooner
Cargo:	Currants
Home port:	Bandholm
Voyage:	London to Celte
Date built:	1876
Owner:	Kromann & Co., Marstal, Denmark
Master:	A.M. Kromann
No. of crew:	5
Ref:	SIBI V2 section 3; HN 1.3.1879; SE 22.2.1879; HC 19.2.1879

The *Appollo* had left London on 14th February 1879 bound for Celte, near Marseilles, southern France, with its cargo of currants. At 3am on Tuesday 18th February in fine weather, when just off Fowl Ness, east of Rock-a-Nore, Hastings, the master suddenly realised that they were a lot closer to the shore than originally thought. In an attempt to rectify this situation he decided to go about but ran aground on the rocks. The rocks caused serious damage to the hull resulting in the vessel filling with water.

The *Appollo* was first spotted by a patrolling policeman of the Hastings borough police force, PC Waite, who raised the alarm. The crew of the *Appollo* had set off distress flares and the lifeboat *Ellen Goodman* was launched from Hastings, under the coxswain Mr R. Roper. Fortunately, as the weather was fine the lifeboat managed to rescue the master and all five crew safely.

It took 12 helpers to launch the Hastings lifeboat who were each paid 4s, as well as six horses at a cost of 5s each, together with the 15 men of the crew who were each paid 3s, making a total cost of £19.3s.

As the wreck was within easy walking distance of Hastings, numerous people came to see the stricken vessel. Two people were extremely lucky to survive with their lives when they were walking under the cliffs to view the wreck about two weeks after she had run aground. As they walked along the beach several tons of the cliff above them came crashing down, narrowly missing the two walkers. This was just one of many such cliff falls that had occurred recently and a newly constructed concrete groyne to the east of Hastings was thought to be the cause.

Edinburgh

Date sunk:	14.3.1879
Location:	Rye Bay, off Dungeness
Type:	British pilot cutter
No. of crew:	4
No. of passengers:	12 (Pilots)
Ref:	FE 29.3.1879; HO 29.3.1879

As this vessel was a pilot cutter, it was a requirement that it should show a white light at the masthead and also light a flare every 15 minutes. On the *Edinburgh* this flare was placed in an iron keg 40ft (12m) above the deck on one of the masts.

At 10pm on Thursday 13th March 1879 William Landell, a crew member of the *Edinburgh*, started his watch. The night was clear, there was a gentle north-west breeze and they were sailing at three or four knots. He had not been on duty long when he first noticed the green light under the bow of an approaching vessel, the steamer *Severn*, a ship of some 1,119 tons belonging to the Royal Mail Steamship Company, under the command of the master, James Lawson.

William Landell was also on watch with the mate of the *Edinburgh* and it was the mate who ordered Landell to light a flare to warn the steamer of their presence. Landell went to the bow and held the lit flare, waving it above his head for several minutes. By this time the steamer was approaching at an angle and was only a couple of minutes away from colliding with the *Edinburgh*. Suddenly the steamer changed course, which meant she was coming straight at the *Edinburgh*, and she ran into her on the starboard bow. It had taken about 20 minutes from the time Landell first saw the *Severn* to the moment of impact.

When Landell saw that the steamer was going to collide with his vessel, he ran back along the *Edinburgh* calling out 'All hands on deck, steamer coming!' He heard one of the pilots on board, William Robert Hood, call out to the *Severn* 'stop her' but by this time it was far too late. The force of the impact knocked Landell overboard but he was later rescued by a boat from the steamer.

Hood, seeing that a collision was inevitable, took to the rigging for safety and he too was later rescued. The master, mate, remainder of the crew and ten pilots took to the two jolly boats on board but unfortunately no sooner were they afloat than they capsized and all were drowned.

An inquiry into this accident was held on Tuesday 25th March and Wednesday 26th March 1879 by the Admiralty Court at Westminster, London, before Mr H.C. Rothery. Mr Bowen and Mr Mackenzie appeared on behalf of the Board of Trade, Mr Cohen QC and Mr Dixon appeared on behalf of the Trinity House Board, and Mr Day QC and Mr Clarkson appeared on behalf of the Royal Mail Steamship Company.

The inquiry took evidence from the survivors of the *Edinburgh* which not only included Landell and Hood but also James Bourner (the cook), Alfred Pike (in charge of the masthead light) and William Charrison (another of the pilots). The inquiry also heard from members of the *Severn*, including the master, James Lawson. He told the hearing that he had been with his employers since 1870 and in that time had passed through every grade as an officer. He said that the steamer was a year old having been built in 1878 and that there were 49 crew and four passengers on board, two of which were children. Of the collision he said that at about midnight his ship was sailing at about nine knots and that he had just been relieved by his second officer, Clement James Bateman, who was then in command on the bridge together with a North Sea pilot, Giles Stringell, who had joined the steamer at Southampton. There was a forward watch and a further one on the lower bridge. He said that as soon as the collision occurred, which was about 2 miles (3km) from shore, his ship's boats had been lowered. He said that about five minutes before the collision his ship altered course which caused him some concern, but the accident happened before he was able to ascertain the reason for the change of course. He told the hearing that it would normally take about 15 minutes for the steamer to make a complete 360-degree turn.

When the second officer of the *Severn*, Clement Bateman, gave his evidence he said that he had noticed the lights of the *Edinburgh* when she was about two miles away. He watched the lights to ascertain the direction of the *Edinburgh* and decided it was safe to go to port. As the *Severn* did so, she struck the *Edinburgh*. He said that it had taken about five minutes between first seeing the

Edinburgh and the moment of impact. He told the hearing that the pilot cutter was not showing any flares. The pilot on board the steamer, Stringell, gave similar evidence to that of Bateman and believed all the proper orders were given by the steamer's second officer.

Mr Rothery said that one of the main facts in issue was whether the *Severn* had kept a good lookout. He said it was clear from the evidence that the pilot cutter was showing a light because it was seen by the *Severn* some time before the collision and yet the second officer took no steps to avoid a collision until just before it happened. He felt also that this, before going to port, was an error of judgement on his part. It was the hearing's view that the second officer Bateman should have reduced his speed until he was sure of the *Edinburgh's* course. The hearing's decision was that no action would be taken against James Lawson, the steamer's master, but the second officer's certificate would be suspended for six months.

Horten

Date sunk:	1.7.1880
Location:	Rye harbour
Type:	Norwegian sailing barque
Voyage:	Le Havre to Frederickstadt
Date built:	1852
Owner:	H.E. Roed, Tonsberg, Norway
Master:	H.E. Roed
No. of crew:	9
No. of passengers:	1
Ref:	SIBI V2 section 3; HC 7.7.1880; HT 10.7.1880

At 1am on Thursday 1st July 1880 when 7 miles (11km) off Rye harbour in a force five south-westerly gale, the *Horten* was run into by an unknown steamer, causing severe damage. Not only were the masts broken away but a severe leak was caused as a result of the collision. The crew tried hard to keep the level of water down but the water rose despite their attempts. The master decided to run the vessel ashore, which he did at Rye harbour. All ten persons on board were safely rescued.

Velocipede

Date sunk:	17.8.1880
Location:	7 miles (11km) off Hastings
Length (feet/metres):	16/5
Beam (feet/metres):	6/2
Home port:	Hastings
Voyage:	Local fishing trip
Owner:	James Roper
Master:	James Roper
No. of crew:	1
No. of passengers:	4
Ref:	HN 20.8.1880; HT 21.8.1880

This sailing boat belonged to James Roper, who was the coxswain of the Hastings lifeboat, and was hired for a fishing trip by a group consisting of William Begg aged 30, a visitor to Hastings, and three youths, Charles Hascke and his brothers Albert and Henry.

At 10am on Tuesday 17th August 1880, the *Velocipede* set sail with these four passengers together with Roper and another crew member, James Hinkley. They sailed out for about a mile and laid out the trawl net, drifting towards Bulverhythe. It was off here at 3pm that they hauled in the net and let go the anchor to wait for the tide to turn for the return to Hastings. It was then that the wind started to freshen and Roper reefed the sail as a result. Initially Roper decided to run to Bexhill because he did not think they would get back to Hastings. However, Hinkley convinced him to try and make as far as the Saxon Hotel, which would be safer for all concerned. When they were off the Saxon Hotel, Roper decided that he would try and sail back to Hastings. By now the wind had dropped and so Roper took out the first of the reefs and after a further 30 minutes of sailing took out the remaining reef because the wind was continuing to drop. The *Velocipede* was now about 5 miles (8km) out and Roper had the sheet in his hand throughout. Although it was not cleated in any way he did have it wound in a half hitch round the crutch. Hinkley was at the bow of the boat as lookout and the passengers were sitting equally around the boat.

At about 5pm there was a sudden gust of wind which filled the sails, so Roper let go of the sheet to steady the boat. Unfortunately this was not enough to prevent the boat from capsizing, throwing all the occupants, except Hinkley, into the water. Hinkley managed to hang onto the boat and climb onto the keel. Two of the youths, Albert and Charles, also managed to get onto the keel. Roper then managed to hold onto the hands of Henry and Begg, but after a short while had to let go of them through sheer exhaustion. Henry Hascke's body sank while that of William Begg floated away from the upturned sailing boat.

Fortunately for the survivors there was a fishing smack, the *La Mere de Saubeur*, under the command of Fairthomine Amone, very close by, and he saw the upturned hull of the *Velocipede*. He dispatched two of his crew in their jolly boat to see what could be done to assist. They managed to rescue those on the keel and recover the body of William Begg from the sea before landing them at Hastings.

The day after this incident an inquest was held into the death of the passenger William Begg, at Hastings town hall, before Mr Davenport Jones, the Hastings borough coroner. The first witness to give evidence was Allan Begg who was a draper by occupation and the brother of the deceased. He said that the deceased lived with him at Jasmine Road, Penge, London and was also a draper by occupation. He said that the last time he had seen his brother was a fortnight previously just before he came to Hastings for a visit with his wife.

The second witness was Charles Hascke who told the court that his 14th birthday was the following month. He said that he was currently a Naval cadet of the Worcester training ship stationed at Greenhithe, London. He told the court that his brother Albert was at the tiller of the sailing boat on the sail back to Hastings but Roper was telling him what to do. There then came the following exchange between the coroner and the boy over the amount of alcohol that was on the sailing boat and how much of it was drunk by whom:

Coroner: *'Was there any drink on board?'* Hascke: *'There was a bottle of gin.'* Coroner: *'Anything else?'* Hascke: *'Three or four bottles of ale and stout.'* Coroner: *'Were the boatmen sober?'* Hascke hestitantly: *'One was.'* Coroner: *'Who was sober?'* Hascke: *'Mr Roper drank a lot of gin.'* Coroner: *'I asked you which man was *sober?'* Hascke: *'What do you mean?'* Coroner: *'Surely you know what being sober means? Were either of them drunk?'* Hascke: *'I don't know sir.'* Coroner: *'What did you mean by saying that Roper drank a lot of gin?'* Hascke: *'I don't know that he drank much – they had it between them. I believe Hinkley had two glasses and Roper had the rest.'* Coroner: *'Did the deceased drink anything?'* Hascke: *'Yes he drank a good drop of the ale and stout.'*

The third witness to give evidence before the court was Albert Hascke who said that he was 11 years of age and agreed that after they had been at sea for about four or five hours Roper had given him the tiller but that he was under the directions of Roper all the time. He also agreed that he was at the tiller at the time the boat capsized. He thought Roper was sober but did not know how much he and Hinkley had drunk because they were drinking the gin with water.

The fourth witness to give evidence was James Hinkley who told the court that he was a boatman living at 3 Meadows Cottages, All Saints Street, Hastings. He said that they had taken a bottle of Old Toms gin and three or four bottles of beer out to sea with them. The deceased, William Begg, had brought some chicken, ham and bread with him.

The last witness to give evidence was James Roper who told the court he was a licensed boatman living at 32 West Street, Hastings. He said that he had considerable experience in manning boats as he had been 9 years in the Merchant Navy, 22 in the Royal Navy and 9 years in the coastguard service. He was currently the coxswain of the Hastings lifeboat. He agreed with how the others had described their trip except that he maintained he was steering the boat at all times and that Albert Hascke only had the tiller while the reefs were being taken out of the sails. He accepted that there was gin and beer on the boat, some of which he had drunk, but said he was perfectly sober. In the *Velocipede* there was a life-jacket and a cork cushion which he felt was the reason why the upturned sailing boat stayed afloat. When the two boys climbed onto the upturned boat with Hinkley he said he was afraid to climb on as well in case it sank. As a result he stayed in the water all the time until the French fishing boat saved them. Under questioning from Superintendent Glenister of the borough police, he said that he had owned the *Velocipede* for six years and that the vessel was perfectly seaworthy, being a registered fishing boat.

The coroner then summed up the evidence and reminded the jury that if they thought Roper was guilty of a criminal act then they would have to return a verdict of manslaughter. However, he reminded them that a simple mistake was not a crime. The Jury retired for only a few minutes and returned a verdict on the deceased William Begg of accidental drowning. However, they censured Roper for being so far out to sea in conditions that were thought inappropriate.

Minstrel

Date sunk:	12.10.1880
Location:	1.5 miles (2km) off East Cliff/5 miles (8km) off Hastings
Length (feet/metres):	21/6
Type:	British Racing Yacht
Owner:	John Howell Jr.
Master:	James F. Swaine
No. of crew:	1
No. of passengers:	3
Ref:	HI 14.10.1880, 24.2.1881; HT 16.10.1880, 23.10.1880

The *Minstrel*, although a successful racing yacht that had taken part in many south coast regattas, was on Tuesday 12th October 1880 taking a party fishing for the day. The yacht had been lent to Messrs Philcox Brothers, well-known pleasure yacht owners, for the party of three who chartered her to go fishing. The party consisted of William Lindsay of 7 Verulam Place, Hastings, Thomas Rodwell and William Docwra, aged 29, a hosier of 37A Robertson Street, Hastings. The crew for this ill-fated trip was Charles William Burton, a first-class licensed boatman of 76 Stonefield Road, Hastings, who had been hired for the trip the previous evening by the master, James Frederick Swaine.

Although it was raining at the time, the *Minstrel* and its fishing party set off from the Queen's Hotel at about 6am in a northerly breeze. They sailed south east until they were off Winchelsea, and then sailed south for awhile before the party started fishing. As is the case with most fishermen, they wanted to try other areas and so sailed in closer to land to a point off Haddocks coastguard station, near Hook's Hard. It was about 12 noon when they dropped anchor and, with the main sail still up and secured fast, they settled down in the stern for more fishing. It was usual practice to keep the main sail up as it steadied the boat at anchor, although during the winter months a smaller main sail was used as was the case on this occasion.

After an hour the fishing party were still at the stern and by this time were eating their lunch. The sea had become quite choppy by now, it was pouring with rain and the wind was very squally. Suddenly a strong gust of wind filled the secured main sail causing the boat to heel over to the port side and start to fill with water at the stern. Swaine tried to release the main sail so the vessel would come back upright but it was too late, and in no time at all the vessel sank, stern first. All those on board were good swimmers except Swaine, but he like the others was dressed in oilskins and heavy clothing to keep out the cold and damp.

Nearby were two local fishing boats at anchor, who heard those on board the *Minstrel* call out for help. On one of these fishing boats with his father was Henry Harman Jr. of 64 All Saints Street, Hastings, who heard the shouting. He looked in the direction of the *Minstrel* to see the vessel half under the water. He and his father then set sail towards the *Minstrel* to assist them. This was also the case with the other fisherman who was about a quarter of a mile away, William White of Scriven's Buildings, Hastings. He also set sail for the *Minstrel* to assist those on board. William Harman and his father were the first to reach the scene and they rescued the boatman, Burton, from the sea. They could not see any of the other people that were on the *Minstrel* despite a search. William White was next to arrive, and he found the body of William Docwra floating in the sea. He found none of the others.

The following evening, Wednesday 13th October, an inquest was held at Hastings town hall, before the borough coroner, Mr Davenport Jones. The first witness called to give evidence was Mr Ashenden, a surgeon, who told the court that it was his opinion that the deceased William Docwra had died from drowning. The other witnesses who gave evidence were Charles Burton, Henry Harman Jr., William White, PC Ward and William Purfield, who identified the deceased. PC Ward told the inquest that he had been notified of the accident at about 3.30pm and on arriving at the beach found that the body of the deceased was just being removed from William White's boat. He took possession of the body and escorted it to the mortuary where, on searching the deceased's clothes, he found a gold watch, 14s.8d in cash, two pocket knives, a pipe, a tobacco pouch and a case. On the case was inscribed 'W. Docwra'. After hearing all the evidence the coroner summarised what the jury had heard and they retired to consider their verdict.

When they returned several minutes later, they told the coroner their verdict was one of accidental death.

On the evening of Friday 15th October, the wreck of the *Minstrel* was accidentally found by a fishing smack, which left a buoy to mark the spot. The following morning, at 10am, Mr Philcox set off in a boat together with two others, intending to see if the yacht could be raised. On arrival at the wreck they tried to find *Minstrel's* anchor by the use of a grappling iron. One of the men engaged in this was Joseph Upton and it was not long before he pulled up the grappling iron only to find that he had caught the body of James Swaine. Mr Philcox and his men then made attempts to try and tow the vessel towards the shore but this was unsuccessful. However, a further attempt was made at low tide and this was partially successful in that they managed to tow it in towards the shore for about a mile. The following day a further attempt was made to bring the *Minstrel* to the shore, which was totally successful and she was beached at East Well, Rock-a-Nore, Hastings. The owner examined the vessel and decided that as it was not too badly damaged and he intended to refit the yacht and hopefully to race her again.

It appears that the passenger William Lindsay was no stranger to the *Minstrel* as he was the owner of another yacht named *Spinaway* and had raced against the *Minstrel* in the Hastings regatta the previous August. On that occasion *Minstrel* beat *Spinaway* into second place. Lindsay left a wife and children.

The passenger Thomas Rodwell had planned to marry a couple of weeks after the date of the accident, to one of the daughters of William Edwards, of the Fountain Inn, St Andrews Road, Hastings. It was understood that Rodwell had arranged to take over the Provincial Hotel, Havelock Road, Hastings after he was married. The master of the *Minstrel*, James Swaine, had also made arrangements to be married within a fortnight of this terrible accident.

Rodwell's body was recovered about a month after the accident on the French coast near Dieppe. A newspaper seller was employed to assist in stripping the body for the authorities, although in February 1881 he appeared before the French tribunal of correctional police in Dieppe, charged with stealing rings from Rodwell's body. Another man named Hayes, who lived at Treport, was also charged with aiding and abetting the newspaper seller. Both men were convicted. The newspaper seller was sentenced to three years' imprisonment and Hayes was sentenced to six months' imprisonment and also had to pay a fine of 200 francs.

Victor Hamille

Date sunk:	18.1.1881
Location:	Wallsend, Pevensey
Type:	French fishing lugger
Home port:	Boulogne (port no. 1244)
No. of crew:	7 and 3 boys
Ref:	LL No. 20820. 19.1.1881; SEA 12.3.1881; EC 22.1.1881; HC 16.3.1881

On the morning of Tuesday 18th January 1881 there was a terrible snowstorm in the Pevensey Bay area and one of the vessels out in the bay at this time was the *Victor Hamille*. The weather was so severe that it blew the vessel onto a groyne at Wallsend, near Pevensey. The crew were almost unconscious from exhaustion because of the terrible conditions that they had been fighting in order to control their vessel.

When they hit the beach two or three planks were stoved in, but the damage was not too severe. The crew managed to blow their warning horn and luckily the local coastguard heard this over the noise of the storm. One of the coastguardmen involved was Samuel Screech, who waded into the ferocious sea up to his waist with a line. This action, albeit brave in the circumstances, was not without its dangers. He was knocked over at least once by the waves and came perilously close to being carried away by the sea, but managed to regain his footing. Having got the line aboard the *Victor Hamille,* the crew were brought to shore safely.

Samuel Screech was later awarded a silver medal by the Board of Trade for his part in this rescue. Around the rim of the medal was inscribed 'Samuel Screech, wreck of the *Victor Hamille*, on the 18th January 1881'. On the face of the medal was the inscription 'Awarded by the Board of Trade, for gallantry in saving life. VR'.

Sophia Holten

Date sunk:	10.2.1881
Location:	Ashore at Jury's Gap coastguard station
Length (feet/metres):	61/18
Beam (feet/metres):	19/6
Type:	British sailing sloop
Cargo:	Grain
Home port:	Plymouth
Voyage:	London to Jersey
Date built, builder:	1869, Westacott at Saltash near Plymouth
Owner:	Mrs W.T. Kelly, Turnchapel, Plymouth
Master:	J.C. Blann
No. of crew:	3
Ref:	SIBI V2 section 3; RNLI; HO 12.2.1881

This vessel was caught in a violent force seven south-westerly storm with extremely heavy seas, early in the morning of Thursday 10th February 1881. The *Sophia Holten* sent up the usual distress signals which were fortunately seen by the Camber coastguard station lookout. It was not long before they had launched their lifeboat and after extreme difficulty managed to manoeuvre their lifeboat through the horrendous surf. However, by the time they were clear of the surf, the *Sophia Holten* had run aground at Jury's Gap with the sea constantly washing over her. For safety the crew had taken to the vessel's rigging. Meanwhile the lifeboat was battling with the sea conditions and weather to get near to the sloop. Ashore, the coastguards of Jury's Gap station had got the rocket apparatus ready and fired a line to the lifeboat. With this they were able to reach the sloop but it had taken five hours of exhaustive effort by the lifeboat crew.

Having reached the sloop they managed to rescue two of the crew from the rigging, one of whom had been struck by lightning in a storm the previous Monday night. No sooner were these two men on the lifeboat than the line from the rocket apparatus gave way, which left the lifeboat adrift in terrible conditions, the master of the *Sophia Holten* still aboard her. The coastguard chief boatman, Mr Dudley, seeing the difficulties the lifeboat was having, decided to launch the coastguard galley to assist. Another line was fired across the sloop by the rocket apparatus, which fortunately managed to grasp the sloop securely enough for the galley crew to use and get alongside to rescue the master.

The local Lloyds' agent, Mr John S. Vidler, attended the scene of the wreck because the cargo was insured with Lloyds. Later, about 60 quarters of the rather wet cargo were recovered.

Launching the lifeboat for this rescue was quite expensive. The total cost was £32.13s.6d. This covered the cost of the 13-man crew at £1 per crew member, 5s. for each of the 15 helpers, 1s for each of 7 extra helpers, 12s for each of the 12 horses used, together with 4s for each of the six horse drivers. There was also an additional reward made to the 13 extra men and 15 extra helpers that were needed.

Juno

Date sunk:	3.3.1881
Location:	4 miles (6km) south east of Royal Sovereign Light
Length (feet/metres):	88/27
Beam (feet/metres):	22/6.7
Type:	British sailing schooner
Cargo:	China clay, gunpowder
Home port:	Fowey, Cornwall
Voyage:	Fowey to Newcastle upon Tyne
Date built, builder:	1864, Slade at Polruan, Cornwall
Owner:	S. Slade, Polruan, Cornwall
Master:	W. Abbott
No. of crew:	5
Ref:	SIBI V2 section 3; EG 9.3.1881; HN 11.3.1881

On the evening of Thursday 3rd March 1881, the *Juno* was four miles south east of the Royal Sovereign Light in a force five south-easterly wind. The *Lady Ruthven* of Greenock was under tow in the same vicinity when she ran the *Juno* down, causing the *Juno* to sink within five minutes of the collision. Three of the *Juno* crew were saved by the *Lady Ruthven* but the other three were drowned, two of them going down with the vessel. The three rescued men, namely the master, the mate and one seaman, were landed at Plymouth on the following Sunday.

Prince

Date sunk:	3.3.1881
Location:	Entrance to Rye harbour
Type:	British sailing schooner
Cargo:	Granite boulders
Home port:	Porthleven, Cornwall
Voyage:	Porthleven to London
Date built	1856, Birkenhead
Owner:	J. Simmons, Portheven
Master:	W.B. Stodden
No. of crew:	4
Ref:	SIBI V2 section 3; SE 8.3.1881

The *Prince* was off Rye with its cargo of granite boulders when the weather and sea forced the vessel to become stranded on the sand bar at Nook Point to the west of Rye harbour. The crew were safely rescued from the vessel, which quickly filled with water.

Coastguard Galley (Unknown)

Date sunk:	8.8.1881
Location:	400 yards (365m) offshore between Fairlight and Haddocks coastguard stations
Type:	Galley
Home port:	Winchelsea
Voyage:	Hastings to Winchelsea
No. of crew:	5
No: of passengers:	2
Ref:	HC 10.8.1881

On Monday 8th August 1881 men from the various coastguard stations in the area were transferring all their old stores to Hastings in their galleys. The transfer had all gone very well and according to plan and by the end of the day most of the coastguardsmen had returned safely to their stations. However, the galley from Winchelsea was not so lucky on its return home.

The galley was about 400 yards (365m) from shore and half-way between Fairlight and Haddocks coastguard stations, when there was a sudden squall. This caught the crew completely by surprise and resulted in the galley capsizing. The occupants of the boat (the station officer, four coastguards and two women) were all thrown into the sea.

Fortunately their colleagues at Fairlight and Haddocks saw what happened and launched their own galleys to rescue those in the water. These, together with a boat from Rye used for carrying stone, managed to rescue all the occupants of the capsized boat safely except one of the men who swam ashore. With everybody accounted for, the capsized galley was towed to the shore and hauled up onto the beach from where it was later refloated.

Friendship

Date sunk:	8.8.1881
Location:	Queens Hotel slipway, Hastings
Type:	Schooner
Cargo:	120 tons of stone
Home port:	Rye
Ref:	HC 10.8.1881, 17.8.1881, 24.8.1881

On the morning of Monday 8th August 1881, the *Friendship* came ashore at the Queen's Hotel slipway, Hastings, in very favourable conditions to discharge her cargo of stone for Hastings corporation. Only 80 tons of the 120-ton cargo had been unloaded when, due to the state of the tide, the remaining load had to be left for the following tide. During this period, as the tide rose so did the wind and the sea got rougher, until by 10pm a strong gale was blowing accompanied by some very rough seas.

It was this combination of high winds and rough seas that caused the vessel's stern anchor to break free. The vessel was thrown onto the beach broadside to the sea, striking a nearby groyne. This caused damage to the stern post and rudder. The crew and those at the scene managed to secure the vessel as best as they could in the conditions.

The following morning, because the weather had not abated, chains were laid out to secure the *Friendship* and make her more steady, while the remainder of her cargo was unloaded. All the cargo except a couple of tons had been discharged by the time the rising tide had reached the vessel again. The conditions were still very rough and waves again pounded the vessel. The coastguard chief officer, Mr Smith, was very concerned for the well-being of the vessel, as it was in a perilous position near a groyne and if the weather worsened there was a real risk the vessel would by smashed to pieces. He sent a telegram to the owner who arrived on the morning train from Rye, together with the receiver of customs from Rye, although there was little that could be done at this stage because of the conditions.

By high tide at 12.30am in the early hours of Friday 12th August the conditions had unfortunately worsened. The sea was crashing over the stricken *Friendship* as she lay on the beach and there was concern that the sea would smash her to pieces. The scene was described: 'The tempestuous sea was a truly magnificent sight, and the grandeur of the scene was enhanced by the fitful gleams of the moon as the hurrying clouds passed over the disc'. However, later that morning, by about 9am the storm had started to ease which was very fortunate because the sea had pushed the vessel to within a few feet of the groyne.

With the weather now improving all the time, a group of shipbuilders from Rye started repair work on the *Friendship* on the following Wednesday, 17th August. It was essential that the vessel be removed from its position because it was obstructing the Queen's Hotel slipway, preventing other yachtsmen and boat owners from going about their business. By Saturday the vessel was ready to be launched but unfortunately the tides were short and therefore did not reach the *Friendship* to float her. The weather over this period had been calm but things changed in the afternoon of Sunday 21st August when a strong south-westerly wind got up accompanied again by rough seas on the high tide. Yet again the *Friendship* was subjected to a severe battering by the sea, and as a result the vessel was moved nearer to the groyne that she had struck originally, which was to be a blessing in disguise, because it was to make it easier to refloat the vessel the following day.

The weather then improved sufficiently for the *Friendship* to float off the beach at 10pm on Monday evening. This was much to the relief of those that used the Queen's Hotel slipway, because they had lost trade amounting to about £50 since the *Friendship* came to grief. Once afloat, the *Friendship* remained at anchor just offshore awaiting the arrival of the Rye harbour tug *Dragon Fly*. However, the master of the refloated schooner, seeing that the weather on the Tuesday morning was favourable and the wind blowing from an easterly direction, decided to sail the *Friendship* to Newhaven harbour and not wait for the Rye harbour tug.

The weather in the early hours of Friday 12th August did not only take its toll of the *Friendship*, but also caused damage ashore, in particular to the old custom house at the east end of Marine Parade, Hastings, which had been constructed on a few wooden piles. The high tide was so rough that the sea soon washed over the promenade and around the base of these wooden piles, which had the effect of loosening them to a considerable extent. The following high tide continued this loosening process on the piles with the result that at 1pm on Friday the building collapsed. Fortunately nobody was injured. The timing of the building's collapse was odd because the man who built the old custom house some 30 years previously, Henry Grisbrook, was buried about two hours after the building fell. The building was due for demolition by Hastings council to make way for a new lifeboat house.

Unknown Yawl

Date sunk:	17.8.1881
Location:	Ashore between Broomhill and Jury's Gap
Type:	British sailing yawl
Voyage:	Erith to Cowes
Owner:	C. Holdsworth, 90 Cannon Street, London
Master:	Thomas Punnett
Ref:	SE 23.8.1881, 27.8.1881; SEA 27.8.1881; FE 27.8.1881; HO 27.8.1881

This yawl belonged to Mr C. Holdsworth of 90 Cannon Street, London, who was on a voyage from Erith to Cowes on the Isle of Wight. The yawl was flying the Corinthian Yacht Club colours. On Saturday 13th August 1881 Holdsworth put into Folkestone and took on board a local man called Thomas Punnett, a widower aged 40, who had a reputation in the port of being the most courageous seaman of the town. Punnett was to assist Holdsworth in getting the vessel to Cowes. By the following day they had arrived at Rye harbour, where they spent some time. On the following morning, Monday 15th August, this vessel set out to continue its journey and made for Eastbourne where it anchored off the shore and Holdsworth disembarked. This left the vessel in the sole charge of Punnett, to continue the journey alone to Cowes.

On Wednesday 17th August a strong wind got up with sufficient strength that it caused the vessel to break from its anchor chain. This was mainly due to Punnett not having played out sufficient anchor chain. Why Punnett did this is totally unexplained bearing in mind his obvious seamanship skills. The vessel then drifted eastward with the wind and was seen to pass Pevensey still adrift and without any sails set. The vessel drifted like this until it was off Hastings when Punnett set the sails and slowly made towards Langley Point. However, the wind had now become a gale and Punnett was clearly having some difficulty in manning the vessel. A larger vessel was passing and offered to take Punnett on board for safety, but he adamantly refused. Punnett continued to fight the weather but was slowly being pushed further eastward. When he was off Rye he was again offered assistance by George Boreham, master of the fishing smack the *Conster*. Once again Punnett refused the offer and this was the last time he was seen alive.

By 8pm that Wednesday evening Punnett had been pushed by the weather to 2 miles (3km) off Jury's Gap. On the shore between Broomhill and the coastguard station at Jury's Gap was a Mr Southerden of Camber. He was watching the vessel struggling with what had by now become quite ferocious conditions, when suddenly the yawl disappeared. Southerden ran to the Camber coastguard station and raised the alarm. The chief officer at the station, Mr Howes, immediately got the lifeboat launched and it went in search of the vessel. The lifeboat was out in the terrible conditions for nearly six hours searching for the yawl, without any success. During this time the lifeboat filled with water three times, which had to be baled out, and by the time the crew returned to station at 2.30am they were utterly exhausted.

On the morning of the following Friday, 19th August, the *Flora*, a lugger from Kingsdown, put into Dover harbour having found the body of Thomas Punnett in the sea off Folkestone. An inquest was held the following morning before the Dover coroner, Mr W.H. Payne, who recorded a verdict of 'found drowned'.

The following Sunday an effort was made by the coastguard from Camber under the command of Chief Officer Howes, and those from the Jury's Gap station under the command of the station officer, Mr Dudley, using the coastguard galley, to trace the wreck by dredging the area. This was without any success but a fishing boat finally found the wreck on the Monday when it became tangled up in their nets. The fishing boat managed to raise it and tow it into Folkestone. It was so badly damaged that it was later sold at public auction for a nominal sum.

It was later discovered that both Punnett's father and his grandfather met their deaths from accidental drowning.

Margaret

Date sunk:	24.8.1881
Location:	20 miles (32km) south of Hastings
Type:	British sailing Brigantine
Cargo:	125 tons of coal
Home port:	Colchester
Voyage:	Sunderland to Treport
Owner:	S.W. Goodwin, Wivenhoe, Essex
Master:	W. Goodwin
No. of crew:	4
Ref:	SIBI V2 section 3

On Wednesday 24th August 1881 the *Margaret* was seeking refuge at Dungeness from a force eight north-westerly gale, when she was struck by heavy seas that swamped the vessel and caused considerable damage. The vessel was totally unmanageable in this condition and the master decided that she should be abandoned, which was done without loss of life.

Jansson Lina

Date sunk:	25.8.1881
Location:	Ashore near Rye
Type:	Russian sailing brigantine
Voyage:	Trouville to the Baltic
Date built:	1872
Owner:	E.P. Akerlund
Master:	J.E. Jansson
No. of crew:	8
Ref:	SIBI V2 section 3; HN 2.9.1881

At 10.30pm on Thursday 25th August 1881, the *Jansson Lina* was off Camber in a strong gale and being driven towards the shore. The crew raised the alarm using distress signals which were seen by the lookout at the Camber coastguard station. The lifeboat was launched and managed to come alongside the *Jansson Lina,* which had by now been driven ashore. The lifeboat crew managed to rescue the vessel's eight-man crew safely and return them to shore.

This was the second time in eight days that the lifeboat had to be launched under the command of Chief Officer Howes. The previous occasion was for the unknown yawl mentioned at page 202. It was with much anticipation by all those concerned that the station was shortly to receive a new lifeboat.

Franc Picard

Date sunk:	27.11.1881
Location:	Ashore near Jury's Gap coastguard station
Type:	French fishing lugger
Voyage:	Fishing out of Treport
Date built:	1872
Owner:	L. Duponchelle, Treport
Master:	L.L. Augustin
No. of crew:	6 and 1 boy
Ref:	SIBI V2 section 3; RNLI; SEA 3.12.1881; HN 2.12.1881; SE 29.11.1881

This vessel is also referred to as the *Trune Ticurt*.

From Saturday 27th until the following Monday 29th November 1881, a terrific force ten south-westerly gale blew, which at times reached hurricane force. It was in these conditions at midnight on the Saturday that the *Franc Picard* found herself off Jury's Gap. The sea was tumultuous and the French fishing lugger stood no chance of surviving these conditions. Eventually at 3am the wind and sea ran the vessel ashore near the Jury's Gap coastguard station. Fortunately for some of the crew, coastguardmen Moorman and Gibbons, together with a local man called Southerden (possibly the same man involved in the unknown yawl sinking, see page 202) managed to get two men and a boy off the stricken vessel. They ran out to the vessel between the waves as each wave receded. The remaining four crew members were too frightened to leave the vessel and were drowned.

The lifeboat was ready to launch but did not put to sea. Nonetheless it took 20 crew members, a total of 28 other helpers, six horses and their four drivers to get the lifeboat ready to be launched. The cost of this was £6.7s.6d.

The same night it was reported that the terrible weather caused the mail cart to be delayed for two hours at Northiam, near Rye.

Sainte Anne

Date sunk:	16.12.1881
Location:	Ashore near entrance to Rye harbour
Type:	French sailing lugger
Cargo:	Potatoes
Voyage:	Pouliguen to Rye
Date built:	1858
Owner:	J.J. Ertaud
Master:	J.M. Leray
No. of crew:	5 and 1 pilot
Ref:	SIBI V2 section 3; RNLI; SE 20.12.1881; HC 21.12.1881

On the morning of Friday 16th December 1881, the *Sainte Anne* was caught in a force nine south-westerly gale and was running for shelter at Rye harbour. Unfortunately it was low tide and there was insufficient water for the vessel to clear the sand bar near the entrance. As a result, the vessel ran onto the sand bar and became stuck. The master, his five crew and the pilot remained on board until the evening tide, expecting the vessel to float on the incoming tide, allowing them to sail the vessel into the harbour. However, the wind increased before this could happen, which caused the vessel to be driven to the east of the harbour.

The Rye lifeboat, the *Mary Stanford*, was launched and the crew were taken off the *Sainte Anne* with the exception of the master who insisted on staying with his vessel although he too was later convinced that he should leave. Two of the lifeboat crew sustained minor injuries in this rescue. To get the *Mary Stanford* launched it took the 15-man crew, a total of 21 helpers, six horses and their four drivers at a total cost of £20.7s.

The following day the insured cargo of potatoes was safely unloaded from the vessel.

Sagitta

Date sunk:	18.12.1881
Location:	Off Fairlight
Type:	German sailing brigantine
Cargo:	Spirits, perfumes, general goods
Voyage:	Hamburg to Campeche
Date built:	1863
Owner:	G. Albers, Brake, Germany
Master:	Behrens
No. of crew:	8
Ref:	SIBI V2 section 3; HN 23.12.1881; HI 22.12.1881; HC 21.12.1881; SE 20.12.1881

At 5.30am on Sunday 18th December 1881, the *Sagitta* was suddenly hit by what was described at the time as a 'perfect hurricane'. It blew the vessel onto the rocks near the Haddocks Coastguard Station where it broke in two almost immediately. This was witnessed by the Haddocks lookout and Mr McFaul, the chief officer of the station, was informed and a rescue arranged. The station rescue team descended the cliffs to the stricken vessel below by rope. On reaching the bottom they found one of the shipwrecked crew, Herman Taxtor, hanging onto their rope. They tried to ascertain what had happened but he was far too exhausted to tell them.

Later that same day through a German interpreter from Fairlight, Taxtor said that as soon as his vessel struck the rocks the crew put to sea in one of their boats. The crew had been rowing for some time when they did a head count and realised that their master was not in the boat. The last time any of the crew could remember seeing him was in the vessel's cabin. The helmsman turned the boat around to go back to the stricken vessel in an attempt to find the master but once it had made the turn it was swamped by the heavy seas and all hands were swept overboard. Taxtor was unable to say how he came to be on the rocks at the bottom of the coastguard rope, as he could remember nothing of it.

During the course of the day the coastguard rowed out to the wreck and recovered the bodies of the master and two of the crew. The following day the body of the vessel's carpenter was washed ashore just east of Pett.

On the Monday the entire stretch of shore from Fairlight to Rye was strewn with the cargo and wreckage from the *Sagitta*. It was not long before news of the beached cargo reached Hastings and numerous people, mainly from the fishing fraternity, were collecting up the various items that had been washed ashore. They were hence known as 'wreckers'. However, it was not long before the coastguardmen were on the scene and recovered much of the stolen cargo. It was reported that if any of the 'wreckers' gave the coastguard any form of trouble they would be arrested and made to carry the cargo from the beach to the coastguard stores, which was quite some distance away.

Mr J.C. Vidler, who was both the receiver of wrecks and local Lloyds agent, arrived at the scene on Monday and took over the supervision of the recovery of the more valuable cargo, namely rifles and undamaged crates and trunks. These were all moved to the store at the customs house in Rye, whereas the coastguards moved the other items to their stations at Haddocks and Pett.

Although the coastguards were successful in recovering much of the cargo, they were not totally successful, because during Sunday night many of the local young men got away with a quantity of the spirits that were on the wreck. This included 'Hollands Gin', which apparently tasted like a mixture of 'whisky and gin'. As a result the coastguard from Ecclesbourne and Fairlight posted sentries at various points to catch anybody taking the cargo and to deter others that might be thinking about it. One such sentry, a small man in stature, challenged a group of drunken men with his sword and searched each one of them. Several bottles of alcohol were confiscated from them but one of them refused to be searched. The coastguard told him he was arrested and upon hearing this the man became subdued and sat down to await his fate. This one particular coastguard recovered over 40 bottles of liquor from people he had searched.

The placing of the sentries was not totally successful because the following morning many young men were found lying about the cliffs suffering from the effects of the stolen alcohol. It was also reported that some of them had drunk perfume, which was part of the *Sagitta's* cargo. It is not known if this was intentional or a mistake. One 17-year-old man called Shaw, a pipe-clay seller who was living at Mr Thomas Dickenson's lodging house in East Hill Passage, Hastings, had been out at the wreck from the Sunday night until the Monday morning, arriving back at his lodgings at 8am, drunk. He was put to bed in his fourth-storey room to sleep the effects of the alcoholic off. However, during the morning he woke up and for no apparent reason other than as a result of the effect of the alcohol, he jumped out of the window of his room, falling onto a clothesline and fencing at the front of the house. Fortunately for Shaw he was found and did not have anything more serious than a few bruises.

Another young man was not so lucky. Seventeen-year old Harry Benton, his brother Edward and a friend named Robert Adams, spent the Monday night along the shore collecting and drinking bottles of spirits that had been washed up from the wreck. Edward Benton returned home to Bourne Street, Hastings, alone but was concerned for his brother from whom he had been parted. He set out to try and find him but unfortunately at 7.30am that morning, Tuesday 20th December, Mr Frederick Paine, of 62 Priory Road, Halton, Hastings, found the body of Harry Benton near Lover's Seat, Fairlight. It appeared that he had been so drunk that he had laid down where he was and died from the combined effects of alcohol and exposure. On the same day the inquest into the death of the bodies found from the *Sagitta* was held at the Ship Inn, Pett before the coroner, Mr Charles Sheppard. The jury subsequently returned a verdict of 'found drowned'.

John & Ellen

Date sunk:	16.11.1882
Location:	Ashore at Hastings
Type:	British fishing lugger
Home port:	Hastings
Voyage:	Fishing trip from Hastings
Owner:	Mr J. Webb, The Lugger Inn, Hastings
Master:	B. Gallop
No. of crew:	2
Ref:	SIBI V2 section 3; HI 23.11.1882

In the early hours of Thursday 16th November 1882, the *John & Ellen* was returning to Hastings after a fishing trip. At the time there was a force seven south-easterly wind blowing. The master, Mr B. Gallop, was just coming ashore with his vessel when the sea took hold of it and threw it against the beach, filling it with water. Considerable damage was done to the boat, and the fleet of nets valued at £100 which were on board were damaged beyond repair.

Achille

Date sunk:	17.7.1883
Location:	Near Horse Rocks, 3 miles (5km) west of Royal Sovereign Light
Type:	Italian sailing barque
Cargo:	Oil, petrol
Voyage:	Buenos Aires to Antwerp
Date built:	1868
Owner:	L. Negretto, Genoa
Master:	L. Negretto
No. of crew:	10
Ref:	SIBI V2 section 3; EC 21.7.1883; HN 3.8.1883

From midnight to 1am on Tuesday 17th July 1883, the crew of the Royal Sovereign Light had noticed a large steamer, the *Glenogle*, bound for China from London, in the vicinity of the Horse Rocks, which were to the west of the Light. At no time while they were watching the steamer did they notice any other vessels in the area. However, unbeknown to them there was another vessel in the vicinity, the *Achille*, which had been run down by the steamer *Glenogle* while at anchor in the dark. The *Glenogle*, once aware of the collision, stopped and rescued all those on board the *Achille* except for three of the crew, whose bodies they could not find. Obviously at this time nobody locally was either aware of this or that the majority of the crew had been saved and were on board the *Glenogle*, where they were later to be put ashore in Malta.

The first that anything was thought to have occurred was in the afternoon of the following day when the coastguard at Eastbourne and Mr Sawdie, the Eastbourne piermaster, noticed three masts protruding from the sea. It was later hotly debated as to why those ashore in Eastbourne saw the masts of a sunken vessel before those on board the Royal Sovereign Light. Having seen the masts the information was relayed to Mr Rudd, of the Albion Hotel, Eastbourne, who was the Lloyd's agent in Eastbourne. Mr Rudd arranged for a boat to take him to the scene to investigate, in the company of a number of local coastguards.

The sea was very choppy and the distance of the wreck from the shore meant that it took Mr Rudd's boat quite a long time to reach it. When they finally reached the wreck of the *Achille,* which was lying in about 15 fathoms of water, there were no sign of survivors and no means to identify the sunken vessel. The vessel was of great concern to Rudd as it lay directly in the path that all large ships took when travelling up that part of the Channel. On his return to shore he informed Trinity House in London of the location of the wreck and the hazard it would be to shipping. They arranged for divers to go down to the wreck during the following week with the intention of blowing it up to remove the hazard. However, when the divers reached the *Achille* and saw that its cargo was petrol and oil the idea was abandoned, although the three masts were destroyed using gun cotton as an explosive.

It was not until Monday 30th July that those at Eastbourne were made aware of the full story surrounding the demise of the *Achille* and the plight of her crew.

Isabella

Date sunk:	24.9.1883
Location:	Ashore at Cooden, west of Bexhill
Gross tonnage:	280
Type:	Norwegian sailing barque
Cargo:	Planed wood, 4 tons of coal
Home port:	Drammen
Voyage:	Frederickstadt to Hofleur
Date built:	1865
Owner:	Messrs Borck & Son of Drammen and H. Peterson
Master:	H. Peterson
No. of crew:	7
Ref:	SIBI V2 section 3; HO 29.9.1883; HC 26.9.1883; HN 19.10.1883

The *Isabella* left Frederickstadt, Norway, at 2pm on Wednesday 12th September 1883 under the command of the master, H. Peterson, and the seven-strong crew made up of Choral Hildal, the mate, and seamen August Otsen, Hans Augensen, Johan Otsen, Teodor Tongensen, Karl F. Matash and Thomas Johannson.

The vessel arrived off Dungeness at midnight on Sunday 23rd September in very thick fog which was followed the next day by a force seven south-westerly gale with driving rain. The *Isabella* was off Hastings when the storm arrived. She was heading east and had come in as close to the shore as the master dared, to seek protection from the storm. However, many of those watching from the beach felt the master had come in too close and were certain that the vessel would be blown ashore. This was later proved to be the case. One of those of this opinion was Mr James Hockless, the chief officer of Bexhill coastguard. He was so sure that this would be the fate of the *Isabella* that at 11.45am he sent a telegram to Mr Thompson, the chief officer of Eastbourne coastguard station, asking him to send his lifeboat, the *William & Mary*, it being easier for the Eastbourne lifeboat to reach the *Isabella* in the prevailing weather conditions than for the one at Hastings, to the east. However, for reasons never ascertained, this telegram was delayed for two hours before arriving at Eastbourne.

While waiting for the lifeboat to arrive, Hockless and his men went down to the beach with surf lines and lifebelts, in readiness to rescue the crew of the *Isabella* should they be washed overboard. Bexhill coastguard station only had a five-oared open whaler, which in the conditions of high waves and strong breakers would have been utter madness to launch. However, many of the spectators who had come to the beach to watch the events taunted Hockless as to his lack of courage in not launching his whaler.

The coastguardmen of Pevensey station had also been watching the *Isabella* make her slow progress eastward close in to the shore. They were also of the opinion that she was doomed and so 11 men from Pevensey took their rocket apparatus with them to Bexhill and collected a further four men from the Kewhurst coastguard station on the way.

The *Isabella* was by now just off Cooden and getting ever closer to the shore because of the effect of the south-westerly gale. The master, Peterson, tried to go about and make for the open sea but the boat in fact turned towards the shore. Peterson tried a second time, again without success due both to the age of the vessel and the fact that it was a difficult ship to go about. The vessel by now had its stern to the shore, to which it was getting ever closer. The vessel was now being blown by the gale stern first towards the shore. At 11.50am the vessel was driven ashore onto the east reef and sandbank off Cooden, in 13 feet (4m) of water.

It was now imperative that the crew stabilise the *Isabella*, preventing her from being top heavy. The crew got their axes and chopped down the main mast and rigging, the bowsprit and jib boom having already been swept away by the sea. The crew then hoisted all the sails on the fore mast and in effect sailed the vessel astern, closer to the beach. It was not long before she became stuck fast, with the action of the sea and gale force winds forcing her port-side-on, towards the beach. The *Isabella* was now in a very precarious position and at the mercy of the raging sea. As each wave broke over her, the force of tons of water rushing across her deck smashed the deck housing, and slowly pushed the vessel eastward over the sandbank. Throughout, the vessel was constantly being thrown about by the waves and was pushed a further half mile along the coast, until it finally came to rest close to the beach. Here, it was protected to some extent from the open sea by the sandbank.

A contingent of coastguards from Pevensey and Kewhurst arrived on the scene with the rocket apparatus nearly two hours after the *Isabella* had first run aground. This apparatus was set up and the first rocket, with its lifeline attached, was fired but did not reach the *Isabella*. This was repeated several more times, each with the same result. One can only assume that this was due to the wind. Those on board the vessel were not really in any immediate danger, because all they had to do was sit out the ebbing tide for eight or so hours and they would then be able to jump from the *Isabella* onto the sand and walk ashore.

Mr Hockless, seeing that the rocket apparatus was not reaching the vessel, sent a telegram to Mr A. Hughes, the station officer of the Bo Peep coastguard station, asking him to bring their rocket apparatus to the scene. The detachment of six men arrived shortly after and, with the assistance of the Bexhill coastguardmen, got ready their rocket apparatus. When they fired their rocket they had the same result as their Pevensey colleagues. It was then that the Pevensey coastguard took their rocket apparatus nearer to the water's edge and fired yet another rocket, their eighth of the day. This was, at last, successful and the line fell across the *Isabella*. The time now was 3.30pm. The crew attached a hawser to the line which was hauled in readiness for the crew to make their way to the shore. However, before this rescue actually started, the lifeboat from Eastbourne arrived on the scene. The crew of the *Isabella* decided that they would rather leave their vessel in the lifeboat than be dragged through the surf by the coastguard in a breeches buoy.

Once the lifeboat arrived she dropped her sail and let go the anchor about 70 yards (64m) to windward of the *Isabella*. The crew then played out the cable and rowed towards the stricken vessel, coming alongside her on the port side. The lifeboat was loaded with the belongings of the crew from the *Isabella,* and at 4.20pm the first of the wrecked crew got aboard the lifeboat. Once all were safely on board, they were rowed ashore. However, the ordeal was not over. On reaching the shore a large wave broke over the stern of the lifeboat, throwing her on her side. Fortunately, as the wave receded, everybody rushed to the aid of the lifeboat and pushed it as far as possible up the beach before the next wave arrived.

Later the lifeboat was towed to the railway station by horses and was returned to its station by train, the crew taking the *Isabella's* Norwegian flag with them as a trophy.

Once ashore the crew of the stricken vessel were taken to the home of Mr Hockless, where it was found that the master who spoke perfect English, only had one arm, having lost his right arm some two years previously. He told Hockless that he had been a master for 15 years, and master of the *Isabella* for the past four months. He was familiar with this part of the English Channel, having been to Poole twice in the summer, but this was not the first time he had been shipwrecked. In fact it was his fourth occasion! He also said that he was part-owner of the *Isabella* but his part was not insured, whereas the other part-owner had their part of the vessel insured for £388.

The following morning the weather was fine, but overnight the sea had pushed the vessel even further eastward and further inshore, such that the wreck was now close to the beach. Upon inspection of the wreck, which was lying on its port side, it was found that she and her contents had been severely smashed and damaged by the sea. The furniture was smashed to pieces and the cook's galley was in total disarray. The vessel was obviously full of water and the pumping windlass was broken so none of this water could be pumped out.

On the morning of Thursday 27th September the crew left to return to their homes in Norway, leaving the master behind to help unload the vessel, which was now in the charge of Mr W. Adams, the sub-agent of Lloyd's at Hastings. A John Webb from Brockley, a contractor who was building the sea wall at Bexhill, and Alfred Adams, a brickmaker from Sidley, were both negotiating for the purchase of the cargo as it stood. However, these negotiations were not successful as on Tuesday 16th October the cargo was auctioned by Messrs Vidler, Son and Clements of Rye. One hundred people attended and paid a total of £500 for the 300 lots that were on offer.

Silksworth

Date sunk:	23.1.1884
Location:	2 miles (3km) south of Rye harbour
Gross tonnage:	255
Length (feet/metres):	105/32
Beam (feet/metres):	26/8
Type:	British sailing snow
Cargo:	Granite boulders
Home port:	North Shields
Voyage:	Fecamp to Blyth
Date built, builder:	1866, Rawson & Watson at Sunderland
Owner:	Manners, Coll & Co., Blyth
Master:	Edward Picknell
No. of crew:	7
Ref:	SIBI V2 section 3; RNLI; HC 30.1.1884; SEA 26.1.1884

On the nights of Tuesday 22nd January and Wednesday 23rd January 1884, a tremendous south-westerly gale blew accompanied by torrential rain. It was in these conditions at 1.45am on the Wednesday that the *Silksworth* found herself stranded and at the mercy of the storm and mountainous seas off Rye harbour. Seven of the crew had taken to the rigging to protect themselves from the sea that was now crashing over the vessel, whereas the master had sought refuge in the cabin on the vessel's deck with his dog. The *Silkworth* was in such great danger that the master, Edward Picknell, a 32-year-old man with three children, showed distress signals which were fortunately seen by the lookout at Winchelsea coastguard station.

While the crew of the *Silksworth* awaited rescue, she took a tremendous pounding from the sea which was crashing over the deck, and eventually this washed the cabin away. The master and his dog were both drowned.

Once the Winchelsea lookout had seen the *Silksworth's* distress signals, the new lifeboat from the Winchelsea station, the *Frances Harris*, was launched under the command of the coxswain, Mr

Burr. The plight of the *Silksworth* was also notified to the Rye coastguard station, who launched their lifeboat, the *Mary Stanford*. The only lifeboat to reach the wreck was the *Frances Harris*, and not until 5am. It had taken such a long time because of the terrible conditions. Having got there, they managed to rescue the seven crew from the rigging and return them safely to the beach at Camber Sands. No sooner had the *Frances Harris* rescued the crew, than the rigging to which they had been clinging was washed from the vessel's decks.

The Rye lifeboat, *Mary Stanford*, could not get near the vessel due to the horrendous conditions. The crew said at the time that it was one of the worst seas that they had ever encountered. The rescue, as far as the lifeboats were concerned, was hampered by the fact that the lights on the *Silksworth* had been extinguished, making it more difficult to see her.

The rescued seamen were taken to the sailors' home at Rye harbour. The home was run by Mr and Mrs Rubie but was funded entirely by one woman, Mrs Lucas-Shadwell, of Woodcote, Fairlight.

The *Silksworth* soon became a total wreck, although luckily it was insured.

To launch the Rye lifeboat cost a total of £23.2s which included the cost of six horses and their four drivers. The cost to launch the Winchelsea lifeboat was £27.15s which included the 11 crew and 22 helpers at the launch, the cost of 12 men to help haul the lifeboat ashore with the rescued crew at Camber (plus their travelling expenses) and the 25 men and the six horses to haul the lifeboat back up upon its return to the station at Winchelsea.

Eliza

Date sunk:	22.5.1884
Location:	Off Fairlight
Type:	British sailing lugger
Cargo:	Granite boulders
Voyage:	Fairlight to Rye
Owner:	W. Clarke, Rye
Master:	J. Igglesden
No. of crew:	2
Ref:	SIBI V2 section 3

This vessel was lost in a force two easterly wind.

Swan

Date sunk:	12.12.1884
Location:	Ashore at Hastings
Type:	British sailing lugger
Home port:	Rye
Date built:	1847
Owner:	Mrs Gallop, 20 All Saints Street, Hastings
Master:	W.H. Gallop, Elder Tree Cottages, Tackleway, Hastings
No. of crew:	7
Ref:	SIBI V2 section 3; HC 17.12.1884; HO 20.12 1884; HN 19.12.1884

This vessel, although 37 years old, had recently been thoroughly overhauled and repaired by the owner Mrs Gallop, who was the mother of the master, W.H. Gallop.

On the night of Friday 12th December 1884, the *Swan* had landed on the beach at Hastings opposite the Fishermen's church at Rock-a-Nore, having just returned from herring fishing in the North Sea. The vessel was being hauled up the beach by capstan in the usual way, when the chain hawser attached to the vessel broke. Unfortunately the *Swan* was not clear of the heavy sea that was prevailing at the time. The waves started to break over her and this pushed the lugger broadside-on to the beach. She soon started to fill with water and it was not long before the vessel became a total wreck, although the masts and rigging were saved.

The *Swan* was valued at about £300, half of which was covered by insurance with the Hastings Fishermen's Society.

Sultana

Date sunk:	13.6.1885
Location:	16 miles (25km) south of Rye harbour
Gross tonnage:	159
Length (feet/metres):	94/28
Beam (feet/metres):	24/7
Type:	British sailing schooner
Home port:	Portsmouth
Voyage:	Portsmouth to Seaham
Date built, builder:	1866, White at Portsmouth
Owner:	J. & T. Ash, Portsmouth
Master:	A. White
No. of crew:	6
Ref:	SIBI V2 section 3

This vessel sank after a collision with an unknown French steamship.

Lewes Lass

Date sunk:	31.10.1885
Location:	Near Kewhurst coastguard station, Bexhill
Gross tonnage:	183
Length (feet/metres):	90/27
Beam (feet/metres):	23/7
Type:	British sailing brigantine
Cargo:	Plaster stone
Home port:	Dover
Voyage:	Rouen to Newcastle upon Tyne
Date built:	1850, Sunderland
Owner:	J.W. Miller, North Shields
Master:	John Foord
No. of crew:	7
Ref:	SIBI V2 section 3; HN 6.11.1885; HT 7.11.1885

The *Lewes Lass* was rounding Beachy Head in a force six north-westerly wind at 11am on Saturday 31st October 1885, sailing eastbound for Dover. The tide at this time was almost at its lowest point and the vessel was exceptionally close to the shore. Those on the beach at Eastbourne stood and watched as it was feared the vessel would come to grief, being so close in. It was not long before this fear was realised. The *Lewes Lass* was just off the Holywell Bank when she ran aground on the sand bar. The sea, at this time, was rather rough and there was a stiff breeze blowing.

The coastguard at Eastbourne, on seeing the vessel run aground, launched their boats and went to her assistance together with a number of local fishermen. When they came alongside it was ascertained that the master, John Foord, was ill and that the vessel was under the command of the mate. At the time of running aground, he had gone below to tend to Foord, leaving the vessel in the hands of his crew. The crew were not familiar with this stretch of the coast, which resulted in the vessel running aground.

The vessel was clearly stuck fast on the sand bar and would not get off without assistance. Foord made a deal with coastguard and fishermen that if they managed to get her off and take her to Dover, he would pay them £75. This was agreed. The anchor was dropped and together with the rising tide the *Lewes Lass* was floated off the sand bar. Once afloat again it was found that the hull had been holed when she ran aground. The pumps were manned but they were not able to keep the level of water from rising, which caused the vessel slowly to sink.

The *Lewes Lass* had managed to get just off the Pevensey Sluice but as she was so low in the water, she was in imminent danger of sinking altogether. At 1.30pm the crew got the jolly boats ready and left the *Lewes Lass* just in time as within a few minutes of leaving her, she sank. The vessel finally settled on the seabed in an upright position, about 500 yards (457m) from the shore.

Ida Marshall

Date sunk:	24.11.1885
Location:	1.5 miles (2km) south of Fairlight coastguard station
Gross tonnage:	1,464
Length (feet/metres):	240/73
Beam (feet/metres):	33/10
Type:	British steamship
Home port:	Sunderland
Voyage:	London to Cardiff
Date built, builder:	1883, Osbourne, Graham & Co. at Sunderland
Owner:	I.F. Marshall, Sunderland
Master:	W. Gonal
No. of crew:	16
Ref:	SIBI V2 section 3

This vessel sank on Tuesday 24th November 1885 off Fairlight after a collision with the steamship *Navigation* in a force two south-easterly wind.

Nelson

Date sunk:	29.11.1886
Location:	2 miles (3km) south of Winchelsea coastguard station
Type:	British sailing smack
Home port:	Rye
Voyage:	Fairlight to Rye
Owner:	R.J.Hoad, Rye
Master:	E. Williams
No. of crew:	3
Ref:	SIBI V2 section 3

The *Nelson* was lost in a force six, easterly gale.

Freak

Date sunk:	24.5.1886
Location:	100 yards (91m) west of Fairlight
Type:	British sailing smack
Cargo:	Granite boulders
Home port:	Rye
Voyage:	Rye to unknown destination
Owner:	R.J. Hoad, Rye
Master:	G. Robertson
No. of crew:	2
Ref:	SIBI V2 section 3

This vessel became a wreck while collecting granite boulders west of Fairlight at 11am on Monday 24th May 1886 and was lost in the force six south-westerly gale that was blowing at the time.

Elsa

Date sunk:	7.6.1887
Location:	2 miles (3km) south of Fairlight
Gross tonnage:	482
Type:	German sailing barque
Cargo:	Resin
Home port:	Keil
Voyage:	Wilmington to London
Date built:	1872
Owner:	H. Bauer, Rostock
Master:	Fretwurst
No. of crew:	12
Ref:	SIBI V2 section 3; SE 11.6.1887; HC 15.6.1887; SEA 11.6.1887

On the night of Tuesday 7th June 1887 the *Elsa* was in collision with a Spanish steamer, the *Marques de Mudela*, when about 6 miles (9.6km) east of the Royal Sovereign Light. After the impact, the *Elsa* sank almost immediately with the crew being picked up by the Spanish steamship. They were later put ashore at Portsmouth and were taken care of by the German vice consul.

The following morning, in a very thick sea fog, a local fisherman, John Sutton, came ashore with the news of having found the wreck of the *Elsa*. The Rye steam trawlers the *Pioneer* and the *Crusader* happened to be at Hastings and when they learnt of this wreck both set to sea to try and find her. This they finally did, but it took them a long time due to the foggy conditions. Having located the *Elsa* they found that her sails were still set. The two trawlers managed to fix two ropes to her and at 11am that morning started to tow the vessel towards the shore. They had only gone two miles when the vessel parted under the strain of being towed and sank in about 20 fathoms of water, two miles (3km) due south of Fairlight.

As the wreck was a possible hazard to other shipping, Trinity House was informed of its whereabouts. They subsequently dispatched a steamer to the scene and sent a diver down to dismantle her.

Charles

Date sunk:	2.12.1887
Location:	Boulder Bank, 10–12 miles (16–19 km) south of Fairlight
Type:	British sailing barque
Cargo:	Coal
Home port:	Littlehampton
Voyage:	Sunderland to Littlehampton
Date built, builder:	1844, Kingston at Shoreham
Owner:	J. Robinson, Littlehampton
Master:	Joseph Gasston
No. of crew:	8
Ref:	SIBI V2 section 3; SE 6.12.1887

At 5pm on Thursday 1st December 1887, the *Charles* was off Fairlight in good but hazy conditions when she suddenly struck the boulder bank nearly 2 miles (3km) off Winchelsea. Fortunately a local fishing vessel, the *Conster*, was nearby and went to her assistance. After about 30 minutes the *Conster* managed to get the *Charles* off the boulder bank. It was then that it was found that the hull had been severely damaged and was rapidly letting in water.

The vessel's pumps were manned until 3am the following morning, when it was apparent that the vessel was filling with water quicker than it was being pumped out. The *Conster* stood by throughout and took the crew off, later landing them back at Rye. The *Charles* finally sank in 22 fathoms of water.

> ## *Juliana*
>
> | | |
> |---|---|
> | **Date sunk:** | 12.12.1887 |
> | **Location:** | Ashore west of Hastings pier |
> | **Type:** | British sailing schooner |
> | **Home port:** | Aberystwyth |
> | **Voyage:** | Fecamp to London |
> | **Date built:** | 1864 |
> | **Owner:** | John Davis |
> | **Master:** | John Davis |
> | **No. of crew:** | 2 and 1 boy |
> | **Ref:** | SIBI V2 Section 3; HC 13.12.1887; HN 16.12.1887; BC 17.12.1887; HO 17.12.1887 |

The *Juliana* left Fecamp, Normandy, at 7am on Saturday 10th December 1887 with the master and owner John Davis, James Stock (mate), Edward Hughes (seaman, aged 17) and the cabin boy George Albert Smith. Before leaving Fecamp, Davis paid for 40 tons of ballast, although the mate felt that they had not been given this quantity. During the night the wind increased, becoming quite strong and with the vessel's complement being short-handed by at least one, Stock was concerned.

The following morning Davis complained to Stock of not feeling well and did not have any breakfast, which was unusual. Davis said, 'Do you know, I heard a strange noise in the hold during the night', and then went to take the helm of the vessel saying 'I feel strange noises in my head and singing noises like the beautifullest music'. Stock was frightened and most concerned on hearing this as he felt that Davis was starting to suffer some form of mental illness. The rest of the Sunday was more or less uneventful, except that Stock noticed that Davis was acting more and more strangely.

At about midnight on 11th December, Stock said to Davis 'We ought to be near Beachy Head. Do you know where we are?' Davis replied that he didn't know where they were and then said, 'My wife told me we were all going to be drowned tonight'. At the time the other two crew members were also on deck and they like the mate were very concerned about the master's conduct. About three hours later the mate sighted Beachy Head, having recognised the light, and he pointed it out to Davis who refused to believe it was Beachy Head. Davis said to the crew, 'I am going overboard so I wish you all good-bye'. He turned to the cabin boy, Smith, and said, 'Are you ready? I am going to leave, will you come overboard with me?' On hearing this, Stock took Davis below deck and managed to calm him down until about 9.30am on Monday morning when Davis reappeared on deck again. This time he accused Stock of having other people on board the vessel because he heard people on board during the night. In order to placate him, Stock took Davis round the vessel to prove to him that this was not the case, but Davis was still not satisfied and returned to his cabin. When in his cabin, Davis kept clapping his hands, reading his Bible and praying in Welsh, but none of the others could understand anything he was saying.

A short while later Davis emerged from his cabin totally naked and started to climb into the rigging in readiness to throw himself into the sea. Stock grabbed hold of him and, with the help of one of the others, managed to get him below and put him in the cabin. However, there was no lock on the door so Stock had to wedge a piece of wood across it and lash it in place. It was while returning on deck that Stock became aware of how close to the shore the vessel was, it now being among the surf opposite the Alexandra and Eversfield Hotels in St Leonards. Seeing the position the vessel was in, he went below again to release Davis as he thought it was best in the circumstances. Once Davis was back upon deck he tried to throw himself overboard again, but Stock was too busy with the helm to leave it, as the vessel was now in some danger from the ever increasing south-easterly force seven wind that was blowing. He had to rely on the other two to coax Davis back into the vessel, which was successful and they looked after him until the *Juliana* ran aground at about 11.30pm on Monday night. Stock had already told the crew that once the vessel was ashore they were to get themselves onto the beach as quickly as they could.

As soon as the vessel came to a halt Stock looked round to find that Davis was just about to jump over the side. Stock grabbed him and they both went over the side together, sliding down a rope and then making for the beach. The sea relentlessly pounded the vessel and slowly pushed the *Juliana* further up the beach at the same time as turning it broadside on. A small fire broke out from a lamp in the cabin when the vessel hit the shore, but this was soon put out by the coastguard who had been present since the vessel had come ashore.

As the *Juliana* hit the beach, a local policeman, PC Montague went down to the water's edge and saw John Davis come off the vessel. Davis asked Montague if he had seen his wife as he had been locked up for hitting his wife and family. The officer was then told of the circumstances of the previous couple of days by the crew. He arrested Davis and took him to the local police station where he was charged with wandering at large in an unsound state of mind. The following morning Davis appeared before the local magistrates, consisting of Councillor Stubbs (mayor of Hastings), Councillor Revill and Councillor Brown. They heard evidence from Montague and from Mr H.G. Shorter, the police surgeon. He told the magistrates he had seen Davis at the police station and that his conversation was totally incoherent. He deduced that Davis was not of a sound state of mind and not responsible for his own actions. Davis told him that his wife had tied him two to three times in a sack and tried to throw him into the dock. Having heard the evidence, the magistrates sent Davis to the county asylum at Haywards Heath.

In the same court the following day a 15-year-old boy named Albert Bailey appeared before the same magistrates charged with stealing a copper funnel from the *Juliana*. He was fined 10s and costs, or 14 days hard labour in default of paying. He was allowed three weeks to pay the money.

At the end of the hearing Mr Glenister, the chief constable of Hastings police, asked the magistrates to listen to what the mate of the *Juliana* had to say about the vessel becoming a wreck. It was at this stage that Stock told them everything that had happened on the vessel after leaving Fecamp.

Sarah & Elizabeth

Date sunk:	1.10.1888
Location:	Off Hastings
Type:	British sailing lugger
Home port:	Hastings
Date built:	1867
Owner:	C. Phillips, Hastings
Master:	W. Phillips
No. of crew:	3
Ref:	SIBI V2 Section 3

The *Sarah & Elizabeth* was lost off Hastings in a southerly, force three wind.

Plover

Date sunk:	11.3.1889
Location:	1.75 miles (2.8km) south east of Fairlight
Gross tonnage:	414
Length (feet/metres):	130/39
Beam (feet/metres):	26/8
Type:	British sailing barque
Cargo:	Coal
Home port:	London
Voyage:	Newcastle upon Tyne to Palma
Date built, builder:	1858, R. Thompson at Sunderland
Owner:	A. Poulson, South Shields
Master:	A. Poulson
No. of crew:	10
Ref:	SIBI V2 Section 3; BC 16.3.1889

On the night of Monday 11th March 1889, the *Plover* was off Hastings in a north-easterly force four wind with clear visibility. Approaching the *Plover* was the steamship *Benefactor* from Liverpool, when for no apparent reason the *Benefactor* suddenly changed course, headed straight for the *Plover* and ran straight into her.

Seven of the *Plover's* crew managed to jump aboard the *Benefactor* at the time of the collision, although an eighth member of the crew, a Norwegian, Theodor Inglebrechtson, drowned during the attempt. The master and one of his officers remained aboard the *Plover* until the steamship sent one of her boats to rescue them. The vessel sank soon after.

There was little damage to the *Benefactor* which continued on her voyage, putting the rescued crew ashore at Folkestone.

Chateau Margaux

Date sunk:	28.4.1889
Location:	8 miles (13km) east of Royal Sovereign Light
Gross tonnage:	4,035
Length (feet/metres):	385/117
Beam (feet/metres):	41/12
Type:	French steamship
Cargo:	General goods
Home port:	Bordeaux
Voyage:	Le Havre to Antwerp
Date built, builder:	1883, Chantiers & A. de la Giro at Bordeaux
Owner:	Compagnie Bordelaise de Navigation
Master:	A. Sensine
No. of crew:	91
No. of Passengers:	1
Ref:	SIBI V2 Section 3

On Sunday 28th April 1889 the *Chateau Margaux* was east of the Royal Sovereign Light in a force three south-westerly wind when she was in collision with the steamship *Manora* of Glasgow, and sank.

Volunteer (RX 248)

Date sunk:	4.12.1889
Location:	3.5 miles (5.6km) off Rye harbour
Owner:	G. Robinson
Master:	Edward Godden
No. of crew:	2 and 1 boy
Ref:	HT 7.12.1889

The *Volunteer* left the Strand Quay, Rye, to go fishing some time after 1.30pm on Tuesday 3rd December 1889, under the command of the master, Edward Godden. The crew consisted of his son Albert, aged 14 years, Henry Gambrill, 22 years and Thomas Morley. They were expected back the following day.

On the morning of the next day a terrible northerly snowstorm blew up, reducing visibility to a few yards. Also, out in this snowstorm were a number of other local fishing boats, one of which was the *Romp*, under the command of John William Gibbs. He was the last person to see the crew of the *Volunteer* alive, at about 1pm.

The *Romp* was returning to Rye with her catch of herring, when out of the gloom of the snowstorm appeared the *Volunteer* at anchor. Gibbs noticed that the *Volunteer* was heavily loaded with fish, and Thomas Morley called out that they were having great difficulty in sailing her. Gibbs asked if they wanted a tow back to Rye but he got no reply and so carried on. About 30 minutes later Gibbs looked astern of him and could still see the *Volunteer*. This was the last time the vessel was seen afloat.

At about 12.30pm the following Friday, 6th December, the *Naomi & Lizzie* left Rye to go fishing under the command of John Nowell. They had not gone far when one of Nowell's crew noticed a fleet of fishing nets ahead of them together with a vessel's sail. The sail had 'RX 248' printed on it, the *Volunteer's* number. Nowell hauled in the nets and found the bodies of Albert Godden and Henry Gambrill entangled in them, so he returned to Rye with the bodies, arriving at about 4pm, to hand them over to the local coastguard.

The inquest was held on Monday 9th December, before the coroner, Mr C. Sheppard. The body of the boy was identified by his mother Mary, who told the court that her son had been fishing with his father since he had left school. At the time of this inquest the body of her husband had still not been found. The body of Henry Gambrill was identified by his wife Rosa, who said that her husband was actually a labourer but had recently started to go to sea to fish as he had been out of work. The inquest also heard from Gibbs who had seen the *Volunteer* at sea and from Nowell who had found the two bodies. Dr Woodhams told the coroner that he had examined the bodies and could find no marks on them, concluding that they had drowned. After the coroner summed up the evidence, the jury returned a verdict of 'death by drowning, believed to be by accident'.

Annie

Date sunk:	15.8.1890
Location:	Ashore at Hastings
Length (feet/metres):	74/22
Beam (feet/metres):	19/5.7
Type:	British sailing schooner
Cargo:	Coal
Home port:	Hayle, Cornwall
Voyage:	Cardiff to Hastings
Date built, builder:	1864, Willmett at Padstow
Owner:	J. Rogers, Swansea
Master:	Robert H. Hoyle
No. of crew:	2 and 1 boy
Ref:	SIBI V2 Section 3; RNLI; HN 22.8.1890; HO 16.8.1890, 23.8.1890; HC 20.8.1890

On Thursday 14th August 1890, the *Annie* arrived off Hastings with a cargo of coal specifically for the local pleasure steamboat *Nelson,* owned by Mr R.R. Collard. The crew of the *Annie* consisted of the master, Robert Hoyle, Charles Phillips (mate), Philip Andrews and a boy, Richard J. Gustave.

On arriving off Hastings, the *Annie* dropped her anchor to await until the following day before discharging her cargo. However, the weather started to turn stormy over the following hours until at the time of the loss of this vessel a force seven south-westerly storm was blowing. There was nothing untoward until about 8am on the Friday morning of 15th August, when the crew found that due to the rough seas and the strong wind, the *Annie* had started to drag her anchor on a rising tide. The master decided in the circumstances to let go of the anchor and to try and go about to get the vessel to sail further out to sea. The *Annie* was unfortunately too close to the shore and had insufficient sail set to carry out this manoeuvre. This resulted in the vessel being driven by the elements towards the shore near the fish market, eventually running aground on the sand in front of the lifeboat house, causing severe damage to her hull.

Those ashore could see that the *Annie* was in some difficulty and the lifeboat crew had already been summoned, but before it was launched a small ferry boat was put to sea by Frederick Breeds, George Craig, Albert Ditton and George Wingfield. They managed to get among the surf and breaking waves but the sea were so strong that the small boat was soon washed back ashore. It was obvious that no such small craft was going to be successful in getting to the *Annie* through the rough seas.

It was 8.20am, and the lifeboat, the *Charles Arckoll*, was launched under the supervision of the coxswain, Mr Paltridge, with a 14-man crew, consisting of, among others, the three men Breeds, Craig and Ditton. The lifeboat succeeded in getting through the surf and breakers with a combination of its oars and the 'hauling off' rope used by the ferry boat, which was attached to a buoy some distance off the shore. The lifeboat then dropped its anchor and drifted towards the wreck, but unfortunately the crew misjudged it and the lifeboat went to the leeward side of the *Annie*.

The crew of the *Annie* decided that they would have to make their own arrangements to get ashore, and so the small dog on board had a line tied to it and swam ashore. This enabled those on the beach to secure this line so that the crew could use it to get ashore. The crew did so, dropping over the bow into the sea. All safely reached the beach at 9am, an hour after the *Annie* first started to drift.

The lifeboat returned to its station about 25 minutes later. It cost £12.12s to launch the *Charles Arckoll* for this rescue attempt, of which 10s went to each of the lifeboat crew, 3s for each of the 28 helpers to get the lifeboat launched and recovered, 5s for the use of three horses, and 13s for the use and repair of a hawser.

The hull of the *Annie* having already suffered damage when she went aground, suffered even further damage as the sea pounded her. This caused much of the cargo of coal, which was mainly in large blocks, to be washed out of the hold to the benefit of some 50 fishermen and boys who were running in and out of the waves with baskets, collecting it.

The crew were looked after by William Gallop, of Elder Tree Cottage, East Hill, Hastings, the honorary local agent of the Shipwrecked Fishermen and Mariners Benevolent Society. He took the crew to the Shaftesbury Dining Rooms, Bourne Street, where they were provided with food and clothes at a cost of £4.7s.8d.

Later in the afternoon, the crew left Hastings by train for the society's headquarters at Dock Street, London, where it was arranged for them to return to Cornwall.

On the following receding tide it was found that the *Annie* had become a complete wreck.

Sudbourne

Date sunk:	24.11.1890
Location:	9.5 miles (15km) south east of Hastings
Gross tonnage:	1,744
Length (feet/metres):	250/76
Beam (feet/metres):	39/12
Type:	British full-rigged sailing vessel.
Cargo:	Salt
Home port:	Liverpool
Voyage:	Hamburg to Rangoon
Date built, builder:	1884, Richardson Duck & Co. at Stockport-on-Tees
Owner:	C.W. Kellock & Co., Liverpool
Master:	J. Macghie
No. of crew:	26
No. of passengers:	1
Ref:	SIBI V2 Section 3

On Monday 24th November 1890 the *Sudbourne* was in collision with another full-rigged sailing vessel, the *Mangalore* from Liverpool, in a force ten westerly storm. As a result of this collision 11 crew were lost.

George Williams

Date sunk:	9.3.1891
Location:	2 miles (3km) south east of Rye harbour
Gross tonnage:	59
Type:	British sailing schooner
Cargo:	Nitrate of soda, 202 barrels of paraffin oil
Voyage:	London to Rye
Date built:	1859
Owner:	S. Wishart, London
Master:	W. Ely
No. of crew:	2
Ref:	SIBI V2 Section 3; HO 14.3.1891; HN 13.3.1891

On Monday 9th March 1891, a force seven easterly gale and snowstorm blew up and one of the vessels caught out in this was the *George Williams*. The vessel arrived off Rye harbour at about 3pm with its cargo destined for the Rye chemical works. However, the *George Williams* had to lie at anchor just off the harbour entrance to wait for permission to enter. Unfortunately, due to the terrible weather conditions, the vessel was blown ashore and quickly started to fill with water once she had grounded. The crew manned the pumps but they were not sufficient to cope with the leaking hull, so the master and his two crew were forced to leave the vessel to the mercy of the sea and weather, by taking to their boat at about 10.30pm.

The crew got safely to the beach where a member of the Winchelsea coastguard station was waiting for them, having seen their difficulties earlier. They were then taken to the local Lloyd's agent, Messrs Vidler & Son, who looked after the men.

Henrietta

Date sunk:	9.3.1891
Location:	Ashore at Bo Peep, St Leonards
Type:	British fishing lugger
Home port:	Hastings
Date built:	1873
Owner:	Charles Phillips
Master:	Charles Phillips
No. of crew:	2
Ref:	SIBI V2 Section 3; HC 11.3.1891; 18.3.1891; HO 14.3.1891; HN 13.3.1891; BC 14.3.1891

At 9am on Monday 9th March 1891, the fishing lugger *Henrietta* left the Stade at Hastings to go trawling. The crew consisted of the master Charles ('Scotchie') Phillips aged 66 years, of Bourne Walk, his nephew George ('Duke') Phillips of Beaconsfield House, Tackleway, and 36-year-old Henry ('Tring') Brasier. When they set off the weather was reasonable, but by the afternoon a terrific gale and snowstorm had blown up. Phillips, being aware of the worsening weather, made for Hastings and arrived about a mile off Rock-a-Nore, at about 4pm. However, because the tide was so low, he had to drop anchor and wait for it to rise in order to get ashore. By the evening the weather had deteriorated and was described as being the worst that anybody could remember. Visibility was very poor due to the driving snow and freezing conditions and the *Henrietta* was riding the storm out at anchor.

It was in these worsening conditions that at 7pm George Phillips cut the anchor free in order for the vessel to make a run for the shore. Unfortunately the weather prevented them from carrying out this manoeuvre and they were driven westwards to almost opposite the Queens Hotel, where the crew dropped another anchor to stop the vessel's uncontrollable drift to the west. An additional problem for the crew was that some of the ropes had frozen solid and could not be pulled tight to set the sails. No sooner had the crew dropped the second anchor than two huge waves washed over her causing the anchor line to break, and the *Henrietta* was drifting, out of control. The master and crew realised that in this helpless state the only place they could safely run ashore would be at Bo Peep, St Leonards. At about 10.30pm they managed to sail the vessel between two groynes at Bo Peep, but each time they got close to the shore the sucking effect of the sea kept pulling the vessel away from the shore, banging the boat against the groynes. It was at this stage that George Phillips tried to throw a line to those on the shore, who were about 9 yards (8m) away, but they were unable to catch it. The constant smashing against the groyne eventually stoved the side of the vessel to pieces. The *Henrietta* immediately filled with water and was thrown across the groyne such that she was floating and aground all at the same time. As soon as the side was stoved in, all three crew were washed overboard but fortunately for George Phillips, who was to be the only survivor, the four fishermen and two coastguards on the beach managed to pull him to safety. The vessel was soon smashed to pieces by the ferocious waves.

A Hastings fisherman, George Sargeant of Brewery Cottages, found Brasier's body the following day at 4.30pm, on the sand at Galley Hill. The body of Charles Phillips was found on the same stretch of beach at Galley Hill at 6pm the same day by a Bexhill fisherman, James Coleman of 2 Hamilton Road, Bexhill. Both of the deceased were married men and Brasier had three young children. The unfortunate Brasier had also lost his father some few years earlier when his fishing boat became a wreck off Sandgate, Kent. The deceased Phillips was the brother of Thomas Phillips of Leon House, Caroline Place, Hastings, who was the proprietor for many years of the Beach Terrace billiard rooms.

The inquest into the two deaths was held on Thursday 12th March at Castle Hotel, Bexhill, before the coroner, Charles Sheppard. The 12-man jury consisted of Mr S. Ockenden (foreman) and Messrs F.S. Cockett, J. Goodwin, E.C. Tickner, H. Rogers, G. Marshall, J.H. Ward, R.J. Cruttenden, N. Gearing, C.A. Talbot, Miles Hampton and O. Hemmings. The first to give evidence at the inquest was the sole survivor, George Phillips, who related how the vessel came to be a wreck. He was asked why the rocket apparatus was not used, bearing in mind it was kept at the Bo Peep coastguard station. He said that he had been told it would have taken two to three hours to get the apparatus ready for use. The two men who found the bodies and then the doctor, Francis Michael Wallis, followed him into the witness box. Wallis said that both of the deceased had suffered blows to the head, which were consistent with having been knocked about by the sea, and it was his opinion that the cause of death was drowning. The jury subsequently returned a verdict of accidental death.

On Monday 16th March, the funeral took place of both Charles Phillips and Henry Brasier together with Henry Adams who lost his life on the same night when his vessel, the *Linnet* also became a wreck (see page 246).

The cortège left All Saints Street at about 1pm to the tolling bells of All Saints, St Clement's, and St Mary Star of the sea churches. The funeral procession made its way to the town cemetery at Ore, through streets lined with almost 4,000 people. There was a similar number of people waiting at the cemetery.

	Linnet
Date sunk:	9.3.1891
Location:	Ashore opposite Marine Parade, Hastings
Type:	British fishing lugger
Home port:	Hastings
Date built:	1881
Owner:	J.J. Gallop, Hastings
Master:	Richard Gallop
No. of crew:	2
Ref:	SIBI V2 Section 3; HC 11.3.1891, 18.3.1891; HO 14.3.1891; HN 13.3.1891

On the morning of Monday 9th March 1891 there were some 39 boats fishing off Hastings when terrible weather struck. Fortunately most of them returned safely, except the *Henrietta* and the *Linnet*.

The *Linnet* was under the command of Richard Gallop of Victoria Cottage, Tackleway, Hastings, and his crew were his brother John Gallop of 69 All Saints Street, Hastings, and Henry Adams, a 20-year-old married man with one child, of 115 All Saints Street, Hastings. The *Linnet* left the Stade at Hastings at about 1pm on Sunday 8th March to go fishing and returned to Hastings about 5.30pm on Monday evening, anchoring offshore. At 8pm they were still at anchor in an ever worsening storm, and like the *Henrietta* they decided to let go their anchor and run for the shore. Unfortunately the conditions pushed the vessel onto the Pier Rocks off Marine Parade, and the *Linnet* was immediately smashed to pieces. However, it took 30 minutes for the master and his brother, with the help of those on the shore, to reach the safety of the beach. Henry Adams got out of the vessel and jumped into the vicious sea but disappeared from view just 20 yards (18.4km) from the beach after three or four minutes in the waist-deep water.

The body of Adams was found the following morning on the beach at Grand Parade, St Leonards, by Charles Mitchell, and was taken to the Rock-a-Nore mortuary. Charles Mitchell was a friend of Adams, and he had left home early that morning to try and find the body of his friend. When he found the deceased his hands were extended above his head, as though he was trying to take some of his clothing off.

The inquest into Adams' death was held on the evening of Tuesday 10th March at the Market Hall, George Street, Hastings, before the coroner Mr C. Davenport Jones. The inquest, on hearing all the evidence, returned a verdict of accidental death.

As described in the entry for the *Henrietta* (see page 243), Adams was buried at the town cemetery at Ore on Monday 16th March, with the two men who died on the *Henrietta*.

The snow was so severe over these couple of days, that the drifts near the castle were some 8 feet (2.5m) deep and a passageway had to be cut through the deep snow to gain access to St Clement's church. The railway line at Polegate was cut off due to a very deep drift, and the Hastings mail train that should have arrived at midnight on Monday 9th March did not get through until 8.30am on Tuesday morning.

> ## *Esperance*
>
> | | |
> |---|---|
> | Date sunk: | 18.9.1891 |
> | Location: | Ashore at Carlisle Parade, Hastings |
> | Type: | British sailing cutter |
> | Cargo: | Cement |
> | Voyage: | Rochester to Jersey |
> | Date built: | 1868 |
> | Owner: | A. Hunt, Jersey |
> | Master: | H. Holmes |
> | No. of crew: | 2 |
> | Ref: | SIBI V2 Section 3; RNLI; HN 25.9.1891; HO 19.9.1891; HC 23.9.1891 |

Early on the morning of Friday 18th September 1891 the *Esperance* was rounding Beachy Head when she struck a rock which caused a leak in the hull. The vessel dropped her anchor and the crew manned the pumps hoping they would be able to get all the water out and so continue their voyage. Unfortunately it soon became apparent that the vessel was filling with water faster than the pumps could pump it out. This left the master with very little option other than to run for the shore and beach the vessel to save the crew. The wind was south westerly and with a strong tide running, the master decided it would be best to run for Hastings. They set the sails and in the strong wind made good progress but all the time the vessel was getting lower in the water.

At about 9am, the vessel passed off the end of Hastings pier where the engineer, a Mr Hawkins, and several of his workmen, asked the crew if they were all right. The crew replied that they were sinking, and so Hawkins suggested to them that they could beach their vessel at the end of Robertson Terrace. Unfortunately this was one of the worst spots to beach such a vessel because the sea washed right up against the sea wall when it was rough, and also there were no capstans on this part of the beach to haul the vessel out of the water.

The duty coastguard at Marine Parade, Hastings, had seen the distress flag being flown by the *Esperance*, and had alerted the chief coastguard officer, Cox, who in turn had alerted the lifeboat coxswain. Its crew dragged the lifeboat, the *Charles Arckoll*, with assistance from the coastguard, to the slipway opposite the Queens Hotel, a process that took just nine minutes. However, by the time they reached the slipway the *Esperance* had run aground on the shore opposite Carlisle Parade. Despite the lifeboat not putting to sea, it still cost £4.7s.6d, representing 5s paid to each of the 13 crew, 2s paid to each of the 18 helpers and 4s.2d for each of the three horses used.

With the vessel on the beach it was not long before the rough seas turned her broadside with the sea constantly washing right over her. Although the vessel was on the beach it was too far from the shore for the crew to actually get ashore in safety due to the large waves and their undercurrent. Those ashore tried to throw lines to the stricken vessel and after a number of attempts they were successful. With a line on board, lifebuoys could be hauled onto the *Esperance*. Ben Laws, the manager for Mr Hutchinson's bathing station at Carlisle Parade, put a line round himself together with a lifebuoy and waded into the sea. The waves suddenly took him and washed him alongside the *Esperance*, and as he passed the vessel one of the crew grabbed him by the hair and hung onto him. They were both then washed under the vessel and when they came up on the other side the crew member was hanging onto Laws round his body. They were both brought to shore safely with the assistance of others on the beach. Laws was definitely feeling the worse for his experience, but seemed to make a miraculous recovery once he had been given some brandy!

Afterwards another member of the crew jumped into the rough sea and soon reached the beach. The third member of the crew did likewise, but was not so lucky, as the sea started to carry him away from the beach. On seeing this, Frederick Breeds, a local boatman and a very good swimmer, dived into the sea and managed to swim out to the man and get hold of him. He then managed to get him back to the beach where a number of others, who were up to their necks in the sea, took the crew member safely back to the beach.

Fifty minutes after the *Esperance* hit the beach, the sea caused the side of her hull to burst open, bringing down the mast, and the vessel started to break up. This was also assisted, one suspects, by the movement of the cargo of cement. It appears that the hull was rotten and by the time the tide had receded, the only thing left on the beach was the keel and one solid lump of cement.

Rye

Date sunk:	20.9.1891
Location:	Ashore at entrance to Rye harbour
Type:	British sailing schooner
Home port:	Rye
Voyage:	Borrowstones to Rye
Date built:	1846
Owner:	J.S. Vidler, Rye
Master:	G. Budden
No. of crew:	3
Ref:	SIBI V2 Section 3

On Sunday 20th September 1891, a south-westerly force five wind was blowing off Rye harbour. The schooner *Rye* was trying to enter the harbour but the wind blew the vessel ashore. All four crew were rescued.

J.C. Pfluger

Date sunk:	11.11.1891
Location:	Ashore opposite West St Leonards railway station
Gross tonnage:	1,000
Length (feet/metres):	210/64
Beam (feet/metres):	34/10
Type:	German iron three-masted sailing clipper barque
Cargo:	General goods
Home port:	Bremen
Voyage:	San Francisco to Bremen
Date built, builder:	1874, J. Blumer & Co., at Sunderland
Owner:	J.C. Pfluger & Co.
Master:	H. Kruse
No. of crew:	16
No. of passengers	4
Ref:	LL No. 16913 12.11.1891; LR. 1891-2.17 (J); MCA; HO 14.11.1891, 19.3.1892; HN 13.11.1891, 20.11.1891, 25.3.1892; BC 13.11.1891; HC 18.11.1891, 9.3.1892, 16.3.1892; RNLI.

Wednesday 11th November 1891 was a very busy time for the Hastings coastguard and lifeboat teams. The day witnessed some of the strongest winds that anybody could remember. They had started the previous night and were probably at their most vicious at about 4am Wednesday morning, although during the day they did not subside much. People were hanging onto lampposts at street corners to prevent themselves being blown off their feet and chimney pots were blown off roofs. It was in this force ten south-westerly gale that the first of Wednesday's nautical mishaps took place involving the *J.C. Pfluger*, which was 145 days out from San Francisco. On board the vessel were the master and 16 crew, together with a male passenger who boarded at Honolulu and a woman and her two young children. It is not clear whether the woman and children were the wife and family of the male passenger or of the vessel's master.

At about 5am, while the wind was at its most vicious, the vessel was seen being blown eastward before the gale, off Bexhill, without sails and dragging both anchors. The vessel was flying the distress flag, but that apart it was clear to the onlooker she was in great difficulty as with every minute the wind blew her closer to the shore. The men of the coastguard stations at Pevensey, Kewhurst and Bexhill were alerted and made for the Bo Peep area of St Leonards, as it was clear that if the vessel kept on its current course it was there that she would come ashore. Likewise, the coastguard stations at Marine Parade, Hastings and Bo Peep were also getting prepared to give assistance. The rocket apparatus was got ready at the Bo Peep coastguard station and dragged to the beach on its wagon by three horses.

Meanwhile on board the *J.C. Pfluger* the crew and passengers had mustered at the helm of the vessel. Every wave that crashed over the ship washed right across the deck with such force that the spray rose right up into the vessel's rigging, drenching the crew and passengers. Eventually, at 9.30am, with the vessel still dragging its anchors, she became stuck on the sand about 300 yards (274m) from the beach off West St Leonards railway station.

With the vessel now stuck on the sand, the rocket apparatus was manoeuvred by the Bo Peep coastguardsmen to the best place for firing, and the first attempt to fire a line onto the vessel was made. Unfortunately the wind was so strong that the line fell some 50 yards (45m) short of the stricken vessel and a further attempt had the same result. A total of 14 rockets were fired before a line was put onto the vessel.

At 10am the Hastings lifeboat *Charles Arckoll* arrived at Grosvenor Gardens under the command of its Coxswain, Swaine and a sub-coxswain, Moon. The lifeboat was launched about 30 minutes later, 300 yards to the windward of the *J.C. Pfluger*, but no sooner was she in the sea than strong winds and the effect of the first few waves hitting her pushed her eastward and back towards the shore, despite the oars being double-manned. The effect of being pushed eastward meant that the *Charles Arckoll* went beyond the *J.C. Pfluger*, so all their effort was to no avail in effecting any form of rescue. The total cost to launch and recover the lifeboat amounted to £29.12s.9d. This was made up of 15s for the 17 crew,

4s.6d for each of the 30 helpers, 10s for each of the four horses that were used and 7s.9d for refreshments on the day, as well as the cost of returning the lifeboat to its station which was 5s for the 13 crew and 3s each for the 30 helpers.

Throughout the lifeboat's attempt to get to the *J.C. Pfluger,* the coastguard had been continually firing their rocket line at the vessel, still without success until the chief officer, Cox, from the Bo Peep station, took the rocket launching tripod under the shelter of a nearby groyne to protect it from the wind. The line was fired again, fortunately for the last time, as the rocket took the line right across the vessel into the rigging on the foremast. As soon as the line was on the vessel, two of the stranded crew climbed the rigging and secured it. On shore the coastguard placed all their beach equipment needed for the rescue at a point directly opposite the vessel and got the crew on the vessel to start hauling in the line, to which rope and blocks had been fixed. However, even this relatively simple operation did not go according to plan, because as the blocks were hauled onto the vessel the sea caused the ropes to twist together. This meant two of the crew from the *J.C. Pfluger* had to climb the rigging to where the rocket line had been fixed to the mast and then slide down this line to free the block by unwinding the ropes. Being suspended like this to carry out such a task in the conditions was no mean feat and it took them an hour to complete. Once free again, the block was pulled high up on the foremast and secured. This then allowed the hawser to be pulled ashore by the coastguard and helpers, but unfortunately the helpers were so eager that they pulled too hard and had to be restrained by Captain Needham and Captain Moore, before they did untold damage. The hawser was finally secured on the beach and the rescue of the stricken crew and passengers could begin in earnest.

When the breeches buoy reached the vessel, the first person to get into it was crew member August Englebart. It was decided by the master that he would be the first, as opposed to the female passenger, in order try out the safety of the breeches buoy before she used it. Having got into the breeches buoy, the first part of Englebart's journey ashore from high up on the vessel's fore mast meant that he was well clear of the rough sea beneath him. However, during the latter part of the journey he was actually dragged, totally exhausted, through the sea until he was close enough for those ashore to wade in and get him. A local man who was watching realised what the problem was and erected two scaffold poles as an A frame to raise the buoy hawser high above the sea at the beach end. This meant that those being rescued were in the sea for less time. With the new arrangement a second man came ashore from the vessel carrying one of the children. There then followed a procession of rescued men and the mother of the children, who, being unable to climb the fore mast to the buoy, had to be hauled up to it by the crew on the *J.C. Pfluger*. The last man to leave the vessel at 4pm was the master.

All those on board the vessel were safely got ashore, although one of the crew sustained a broken leg getting off the vessel. He was taken to the East Sussex hospital in a cab for treatment. The rest were taken care of by Mr W.H. Gallop, the local agent of the Shipwrecked Mariners Society, who took some of them to the Wilton House rest home, Grosvenor Gardens, St Leonards, and others to adjacent houses.

Once ashore the master refused help from Mr Collard, the owner of the steamer *Nelson,* to get the vessel pulled off the sand. He wanted to wait until he had heard from the owners in Germany. However, in the meantime the vessel was being pushed further eastward by the action of both sea and wind and by the following day was 250 yards (228m) further east. It was agreed by the owners to try and float the vessel off the sand the following Tuesday using four tugs who, if successful, would be paid 1,000 guineas. It was a worthwhile enterprise as the cargo and vessel were valued at about £20,000, but if unsuccessful they would be paid nothing. Mr Cullin of Dover made several attempts to float the vessel without any success at all, despite putting a centrifugal pump in the vessel to pump out some of the water. It was very fortunate that the vessel remained upright from the very moment she came ashore. It was felt that the cargo would have to be removed before the vessel could be floated from the sand.

As can be imagined, such a rescue caused much attention and hundreds of people came to the scene to watch the events, arriving by every train that stopped at West St Leonards station. The 5pm train arrived with still more spectators, even though the crew had by this time been rescued. Among those from Bexhill who had come to watch were Viscount and Lady Cantelupe and Lady Indina Brassey.

On 17th March 1892 a meeting was held at the Fisherman's

Institute, Hastings, by the mayor, Alderman Tree. The meeting was to discuss the distribution of £50 that had been sent to the mayor by the owners of the *J.C. Pfluger*. The accompanying letter read as follows:

Bremen
3rd March 1892

Sir,

Having learned from Captain H. Kruse, of our barque, J.C. Pfluger, *which vessel came ashore at your place on the 11th of November 1891, all particulars and circumstances of the gallant and brave rescue of the passengers and crew of the said vessel, we now take the liberty to request your kindness to tender our sincerest thanks to all those who have rendered their active assistance under such severe circumstances and who have shown a hospitality which will always be gratefully remembered by the rescued.*

We hereby enclose £50 (H56 72105 to 9, 5 notes of £10), leaving it quite to your consideration to distribute the amount to those as you will deem fit for recognition from our part and as a token of our gratitude.

We have the honour to be Sir,
Yours respectfully,
J.C. PFLUGER & Co.

The meeting had been called because £36 had already been raised locally and distributed to the lifeboat crew and coastguardsmen who had operated the rocket apparatus. However, an oversight at the time meant that when this money was divided there were others who were worthy of receiving some of it but had not. The meeting therefore had to decide how to distribute the £50. The mayor was supported by the Revs. M. Edwards (chaplain of the Fishermen's church), H.B. Foyster and F.J. Swanston (St Clements church), Councillor Eaton, Councillor Hutchings (secretary of the lifeboat), W.H. Gallop (local agent of the Shipwrecked Mariners Society), Captain M. Breach and Messrs J. Sutton and Griffin. The meeting finally decided that there were 98 men who were deserving of receiving monies. Those who had already received money, (i.e. 10s) would receive a further 5s and those who had received nothing so far would get 15s each.

Nerissa

Date sunk:	11.11.1891
Location:	Ashore at Castle Rocks, Hastings, opposite Marine Parade
Gross tonnage:	117
Length (feet/metres):	85/26
Beam (feet/metres):	22/6.7
Type:	British sailing schooner
Cargo:	Slates
Home port:	Aberystwyth
Voyage:	Port Madoc to Stettin
Date built, builder:	1878, Thomas & Jones at Aberystwyth
Owner:	D.C. Roberts, Aberystwyth
Master:	D. Jenkins
No. of crew:	3 and 1 boy
Ref:	SIBI V2 Section 3; HC 18.11.1891; HN 13.11.1891

It took until after 4pm on Wednesday 11th November 1891 to rescue all those on the stricken vessel *J.C. Pfluger* (see page 251), and no sooner had this been completed successfully than the *Nerissa* was seen off Eversfield Place, St Leonards, at about 6.30pm flying a distress flag.

The *Nerissa's* problems started at about 2am in the morning, while off Beachy Head. The vessel had been caught in the horrendous storm of that night and while passing Beachy Head had been struck by some huge waves with such force that they caused the vessel to leak. The crew manned the pumps only to find that they were totally unworkable. As the vessel filled with water it made it more and more difficult to sail her properly. The master and his crew spent the whole of the day struggling with the vessel in these terrible conditions. However, they eventually managed to get in close and at about 7pm she ran aground opposite Marine Parade, Hastings, about 50 yards (45m) from the shore having followed the instructions of those on the beach as to the best place to come in. As the wind drove the vessel through the waves and surf, the crew had to climb the rigging to prevent themselves from being washed overboard as the sea crashed over the vessel's deck.

Even though the wind had abated by this time, the sea and the surf were still incredibly rough and no sooner had the vessel struck the shore than the sea turned her broadside-on. In this position the waves beat over the vessel tearing the sails and snapping the fore top mast which fell over the side of the boat.

Neither the lifeboat nor the rocket apparatus were available to help, although in such circumstances the lifeboat would have been of little use, as the *Nerissa* was too close in to shore with just very rough surf between it and the beach. Nevertheless, by the time the *Nerissa* ran aground the local coastguard, together with the fishermen, were already on the beach waiting to get the surf lines ready. They had only just completed the rescue of the crew from the *J.C. Pfluger* and were still in their wet clothes. The only problem now was to get the surf line aboard the *Nerissa*. This was only achieved by the courage of one local man who waded into the sea with the line and managed to get it onto the vessel. The crew then took it in turns to be hauled ashore in a breeches buoy. The last to leave the vessel was the master who, upon getting into the breeches buoy, jumped over the side of the *Nerissa* just as a large wave struck the vessel's hull. This caused the vessel to roll over onto its side and the master disappeared from the view of those ashore. There was, for a short while, great concern for the elderly master as the vessel may have rolled onto him. Suddenly he was seen being lifted on top of a wave and some 20 men on the beach ran into the sea and pulled him safely ashore albeit in a semi-conscious state.

Once ashore Mr W.H. Gallop, the local agent for the Shipwrecked Mariners Society, took care of the master and his crew. The master was later to say that during his career he had been a cod fisherman for ten years off Newfoundland and that he had also been across the Atlantic Ocean twice in the *Nerissa*. Other information he gave included having once been run down by a man o'war while in the Mediterranean. It also transpired that the *Nerissa* had recently been re-classed at Lloyd's for a further nine years, after having had £200 spent on her. Of the conditions on 11th November, he said they were the worst he had ever encountered.

The following morning found the *Nerissa* more or less in the same position, except that it was well and truly stuck fast in the sand. Luckily the actions of the sea had caused little damage to the hull, although the deck and bulwarks were severely damaged. It was then the task of the crew to remove the cargo. This had only been partly done by the time the next incoming tide had arrived, accompanied by an ever increasing wind, and by 7.30pm that evening these had almost completely destroyed the ship.

Warwickshire

Date sunk:	29.12.1891
Location:	Off Camber
Gross tonnage:	646
Cargo:	General goods
Home port:	London
Voyage:	London to Mauritius
No. of crew:	18
Ref:	SIBI V2 Section 3; RNLI; SEA 12.3.1892; HC 3.2.1892; HN 5.2.1892

The *Warwickshire* left London on Boxing Day, Saturday 26th December 1891, for Mauritius. On the following Tuesday the vessel ran aground off Camber in bad weather because the master had not been told by the mate that they were in shallow waters. Having become stranded, the Winchelsea lifeboat put off and rescued the crew except for the master who stayed with his vessel until some time later, when he rowed himself ashore.

On Tuesday 2nd February 1892 a Board of Trade inquiry was held into the circumstances of how the *Warwickshire* ran aground. The hearing was told that she was subsequently towed to Dover by two tugs called the *Lady Beta* and the *Crusader*. After hearing all the evidence the inquiry concluded that although there was no blame attached to the master, he was guilty of an error of judgement. Similarly the mate was also found to have made an error of judgement in that he had not informed the master that he had a sounding of only ten fathoms just prior to the vessel running aground. The inquiry took no further action.

Subsequent to the inquiry there was a court case on 5th March 1892 before the Queen's Bench Admiralty Division, presided over by Mr Justice Jeune. This hearing was to decide compensation for salvage of the *Warwickshire,* valued at about £8,000, and heard a slightly different story: the 18 ton Walmer lugger the *Golden Horn* was claiming compensation for salvage services to the *Warwickshire*. The court was told that due to the bad weather approaching the area around Dungeness, the crew of the *Golden Horn* had set sail for the area searching for vessels that may need their assistance. On the morning of Thursday 31st December the crew came across the *Warwickshire* which appeared, to them, to be abandoned. Having found the vessel the *Golden Horn* went to find help from the steam tugs *Anglia* and *Robert Bruce*, and with their help towed the *Warwickshire* to Tilbury Docks. The owners of the *Warwickshire* said that she had not been abandoned but had only been temporarily left by the crew to get new hands while the vessel was at anchor. The judge gave his findings that the salvage *'was a meritorious salvage, rendered with great risk and bravery whilst great credit was due to the lugger'*. He awarded £750 to the *Golden Horn* and the *Anglia* and *Robert Bruce* shared £2,250.

Speedwell

Date sunk:	1.2.1892
Location:	1,200 yards (1097m) west of Jury's Gap coastguard station.
Type:	British sailing schooner
Cargo:	Oilcake, beans
Home port:	Goole
Voyage:	Goole to Poole
Date built:	1866
Owner:	J.T. Larvent
Master:	J.T. Larvent
No. of crew:	4
Ref:	SIBI V2 Section 3; RNLI; SEA 6.2.1892

The *Speedwell* ran aground at 1am on Monday 1st February 1892 in a force six south-westerly wind. The alarm was raised and the lifeboat was got ready and taken along the shore by two horses to a point near the vessel, where it was launched at about 1.30am. Unfortunately the tide had ebbed to such an extent that by the time the lifeboat arrived alongside the vessel, they were unable to reach her. It took the lifeboat until 4.30am to get back to station at a cost of £17.12s.6d in expenses.

Achille

Date sunk:	11.3.1892
Location:	1 mile (1.6km) south of Royal Sovereign Light
Type:	French sailing brigantine
Cargo:	Zinc ore
Date built:	1870
Owner:	A. Delrue, Dunkirk
Master:	Bernard
No. of crew:	8
Ref:	SIBI V2 Section 3

This vessel was in collision with the steamship *Rameh*, of Liverpool, on Friday 11th March 1892, in force five north-westerly gale, when one mile south of the Royal Sovereign Light. Five members of the eight-man crew from the *Rameh* lost their lives.

Mariner

Date sunk:	9.3.1893
Location:	5 miles (8km) east of Royal Sovereign Light
Gross tonnage:	298
Length (feet/metres):	119/36
Beam (feet/metres):	26/8
Type:	British sailing brigantine
Home port:	Newhaven
Voyage:	Newhaven to South Shields
Date built, builder:	1871, May at Shoreham, Sussex
Owner:	J.H. Bull *et al.*, Newhaven, East Sussex
Master:	C. Care
No. of crew:	7
Ref:	SIBI V2 Section 3; BC 17.3.1893

The *Mariner* left Newhaven during Wednesday 8th March 1893 with her crew of eight. The vessel had not got far before the weather, although calm, became very foggy indeed. At about 3am the next morning the *Mariner* was 5 miles (8km) east of the Royal Sovereign Light in the thick fog, when the master heard the foghorn of a vessel nearby. The *Mariner* replied to alert the nearby vessel of her presence. The foghorn of the other vessel was heard continuously for about ten minutes when suddenly out of the fog appeared the 2,000-ton Dutch steamship *Hispania*. The steamship struck the *Mariner* on the port side, smashing the foremast and causing so much damage to her that it was clear she would sink very quickly as a result. The master and crew managed to get aboard the *Hispania* which was bound for Spain from London, although there was not enough time to rescue any of their belongings. They were not long aboard the *Hispania* when the *Mariner* sank in very deep water, with little hope of salvage.

The *Hispania* carried on its voyage down the English Channel and were about 12 miles (19km) off Brighton when they came across a fishing smack. The *Mariner* crew were then transferred to the fishing smack and taken back into Newhaven.

Nifa

Date sunk:	14.9.1893
Location:	8 miles (13km) south of Hastings
Gross tonnage:	473
Length (feet/metres):	170/52
Beam (feet/metres):	26/8
Type:	Danish steamship
Home port:	Copenhagen
Voyage:	Poole to Blyth
Date built, builder:	1879, H. McIntyre & Co. at Paisley
Owner:	H. Svarrer & Co., Copenhagen
Master:	C.T. Westagaard
No. of crew:	12
Ref:	SIBI V2 Section 3; HN 22.9.1893; HC 20.9.1893

At about midnight on Thursday 14th March 1893 the Danish steamship *Nifa* was steaming up the Channel, 6 miles (9.6km) east of the Royal Sovereign Light, when the crew saw the light of another steamship approaching them. There was also a sailing ship between the two steamers. The master of the *Nifa* steered a course past the sailing vessel and had only just cleared her when the other steamship, trying to cross her bows, ran into the *Nifa* near the middle of the starboard side. The other steamship struck the *Nifa* with such force that it cut a great hole in the middle of the deck.

The master quickly assessed the situation and it was obvious that the *Nifa* was not going to survive this collision. The crew got into their boat and quickly rowed away from the stricken vessel to avoid the suction effect when she went down. The crew in their little boat watched as the *Nifa* went down only five minutes after they had got clear of her. The vessel went down bow first causing the stern to rise right up in the air, clear of the water.

The passenger steamer, name unknown, stopped for a short while but appears to have done nothing to check on the *Nifa* nor its crew. It then carried on its voyage.

The master of the *Nifa* and his twelve man crew started to row their boat towards Hastings which was about eight miles (13km) north of the collision. They eventually arrived at Hastings pier where they were met by local coastguards who took them to the Shaftesbury Dining Rooms, Bourne Street owned by Mr Richard Wood. The local agent of the Shipwrecked Mariners Society, Mr W.H. Gallop, looked after their needs and arranged clothing for them.

The crew remained in Hastings until Friday evening when Mr Gallop gave them rail tickets for the 6.40pm train to London. However, before they left the crew made statements to the local customs personnel at the Marine Parade coastguard station, where the master maintained that he was on the right course and that it was the unknown passenger steamer that was at fault and the cause of the collision.

Anna Maria

Date sunk:	6.2.1894
Location:	Between Martello Tower nos 35 and 36
Gross tonnage:	185
Length (feet/metres):	89/27
Beam (feet/metres):	25/75
Type:	Russian sailing schooner
Cargo:	Minerals
Home port:	Riga
Voyage:	Amsterdam to Barcelona
Date built, builder:	1887, Adosepp at Vpesgriwi
Owner:	J. Stahl, Kurland, Russia
Master:	M.F. Martinkohn
No. of crew:	5
Ref:	SIBI V2 Section 3; SE 10.2.1894; MCA; HN 9.12.1894

On the evening of Tuesday 6th February 1894, there was a very strong south-westerly gale blowing, reaching force nine at times, and the unfortunate Russian schooner *Anna Maria* was caught in it just off Dungeness. The vessel was going down the Channel bound for Barcelona when, as she passed Dungeness, she found herself closer inshore than was desirable and among the surf. The crew tried desperately to steer the vessel clear of the surf but the rough sea, coupled with the wind, caused the helm to have no effect whatsoever. The ship was driven aground in driving rain between Martello Towers 35 and 36 at Pett, about 100 yards (91m) from the shore.

At 11.25pm the coastguards from the Haddocks and Pett stations were on the scene, together with the rocket apparatus from the Pett station. The rocket apparatus was soon ready and under the command of the chief boatman from Pett, Mr Donovan, the rocket was fired. Fortunately the first rocket was all that was required as it reached the *Anna Maria* and the crew made fast the line. It was also fortunate that the Russian crew were familiar with this type of rescue equipment and knew exactly what to do once the line was on board. When the crew were all safely ashore they were taken to the Ship Inn at Pett to recover from their ordeal.

The following tides soon turned the *Anna Maria* broadside to the sea, with the inevitable result that the constant pounding of the waves caused much damage to the vessel, eventually breaking her back. The cargo of minerals (a type of sand used in the casting of iron goods) was unfortunately ruined by the sea, although the following day the crew managed to recover much of the stores and other tackle.

On Thursday 8th February, the weather was very much improved with quite warm sunshine. This allowed many visitors from Hastings to travel to the scene and view the wrecked *Anna Maria* which was about 6 miles (9.6km) from Hastings and about 3 miles (5km) from Winchelsea.

Sweet Hope

Date sunk:	20.12.1894
Location:	Four miles (6km) south west of Rye
Type:	British sailing fishing smack
Owner:	W.E. Colebrook, Rye
Master:	George Buckland
No. of crew:	1 and 1 boy
Ref:	SIBI V2 Section 3; HO 22.12.1894

At 5am on Thursday 20th December 1894, the fishing smack *Sweet Hope* left Rye harbour to go fishing. The crew consisted of the master, George Buckland, and two hands, John Brett and a boy called Charles Sands from Eastbourne.

During the afternoon a northerly force nine gale blew up and it was in these conditions that the tragedy happened. The *Sweet Hope* was trawl fishing when a Norwegian barque of some 700 tons, called the *Kongasgaard*, literally ran right over the top of her, crushing her to pieces. The *Kongasgaard* did stop for a short while but did not offer any assistance to the stricken crew.

Fortunately there was another fishing smack nearby, the *XL* under the command of a Mr Ford and crewed by his son W.J. Ford with H. Tiltman. They quickly made for the accident where they found the boy, Sands. They could not find the other two crew members. Sands told them that he last saw Buckland clinging to the broken mast and was trying to swim towards him when he was picked up by the *XL*. Sands did not recall seeing Brett at all after the collision.

John Brett had only been married the previous Sunday to a Miss Pettit from Iden, and lived opposite the Ship Inn, The Strand, Rye. Brett was the sixth member of his family to die within the previous 13 months.

Guiseppe

Date sunk:	23.3.1895
Location:	11 miles (17km) south east of Royal Sovereign Light
Gross tonnage:	1,010
Length (feet/metres):	180/55
Beam (feet/metres):	33/10
Type:	Italian sailing barque
Cargo:	Resin
Home port:	Palermo
Voyage:	Savannah to Hamburg
Date built, builder:	1886, M.A. Paturzo at Cassano, Italy
Owner:	C. Mazzarino, Palermo
Master:	A. Lauro
No. of crew:	13
Ref:	SIBI V2 Section 3

On Saturday 23rd March 1895, when about 11 miles (17km) south east of the Royal Sovereign Light in a force five south-westerly wind, the *Guiseppe* was run down by the steamship *Storm King*, of London.

Olaf Trygvasson

Date sunk:	17.11.1896
Location:	Off Hastings
Gross tonnage:	883
Length (feet/metres):	175/53
Beam (feet/metres):	33/10
Type:	Norwegian sailing barque
Cargo:	Wood
Home port:	Tonsberg
Voyage:	Gefle to Port Natal
Date built, builder:	1876, T. Tonning at Stavanger
Owner:	J. Bull
Master:	M. Gjertsen
No. of crew:	14
Ref:	SIBI V2 Section 3

On Tuesday 17th November 1896, the *Olaf Trygvasson* collided with the steamship *Balderton* of West Hartlepool in a force five south-easterly wind off Hastings.

Frank

Date sunk:	4.7.1897
Location:	Off Hastings
Type:	British barge
Cargo:	Coal
Home port:	Shoreham
Voyage:	Tilbury Docks to Shoreham
Date built:	1872
Owner:	Artillery Cement Co., Shoreham
Master:	E.F. McNeale
No. of crew:	1
Ref:	SIBI V2 Section 3

On Sunday 4th July 1897 while off Hastings this vessel was lost in a force seven north-westerly gale.

Peter Varkevisser

Date sunk:	8.8.1897
Location:	4 miles (6km) east of Royal Sovereign Light
Gross tonnage:	69
Length (feet/metres):	72/22
Beam (feet/metres):	19/5
Type:	British sailing ketch
Cargo:	Cement
Home port:	Caernarfon
Voyage:	Norfleet to Barry
Date built, builder:	1875, W.T. McCann at Kingston-upon-Hull
Owner:	H. Jones, Portmadoc
Master:	J. Evans
No. of crew:	3
Ref:	SIBI V2 Section 3

On Sunday 8th August 1897 this ship sank east of the Royal Sovereign Light after being in a collision with the steamship *Boileau* of Cardiff.

Lepanto

Date sunk:	6.1.1898
Location:	3.25 miles (5.2km) south east of Fairlight, 7 miles (11km) off Pett
Gross tonnage:	2,278
Length (feet/metres):	303/92
Beam (feet/metres):	36/11
Type:	British steamship
Home port:	Hull
Voyage:	Boston, Massachusetts, to Hull
Date built, builder:	1877, Earles & Co. at Hull
Owner:	T. Wilson & Sons, Co. Ltd., Hull
Master:	J. Bearpark
No. of crew:	32
Ref:	SIBI V2 Section 3; HC 12.1.1898; HN 14.1.1898

On the night of Thursday 6th January 1898, the weather was very foggy and it was in these thick and murky conditions that the steamship *Lepanto* and another steamship, the *Knight of St George*, collided. The *Knight of St George* of Liverpool was on a voyage from Hull to Cardiff and as soon as the collision occurred she stopped and safely rescued all the crew of the *Lepanto*, putting them ashore at her Cardiff destination.

The first that anyone locally was aware that such a collision had taken place was on the following Saturday when the local steam tug *Pioneer* of Rye put into Hastings and informed William Adams, the Hastings agent for Vidler & Sons. The crew gave details of having come across the masts of the *Lepanto* which were sticking clear of the water by some 20 feet (6m) and that another local vessel, the fishing smack *Romp*, also of Rye, had buoyed the wreck. Lights were later fixed to the mastheads to warn other shipping of the hazard.

Pontos

Date sunk:	31.3.1899
Location:	East of Royal Sovereign Light
Gross tonnage:	2,710
Length (feet/metres):	300/91
Beam (feet/metres):	42/13
Type:	German steamship
Cargo:	164 head of cattle, 970 head of sheep
Home port:	Hamburg
Voyage:	Buenos Aires to Deptford, London
Date built, builder:	1885, Richardson Duck & Co. at Stockton-on-Tees
Owner:	A.C. de Freitas & Co., Hamburg
Master:	Julius Terchan
No. of crew:	38
No. of passengers	5
Ref:	SIBI V2 Section 3; LL No. 19208. 1.4.1899; LR. 1899-1900.542 (P); HN 7.4.1899; EG 5.4.1899; HO 3.4.1899

The *Pontos* left Buenos Aires 29 days prior to this collision with a cargo of live animals and two passengers. She steamed up to Rio Grande where a further three passengers were taken on board, before setting out for London. During the early hours of Friday 31st March 1899 the *Pontos* encountered thick fog in the English Channel.

Having entered the Channel, the *Pontos* reduced her speed considerably due to the very poor visibility and was constantly sounding its ship's foghorn. As the vessel approached the Royal Sovereign Light another foghorn could be heard in the distance, but its sound increased quite quickly, indicating that the approaching vessel was travelling at a fast speed. Suddenly, at 9.15pm, the *Star of New Zealand* loomed out of the fog on the port side. Julius Terchan, the master of the *Pontos*, ordered 'Full steam ahead' but this was of no avail as the *Star of New Zealand* struck the *Pontos* amidships in front of the bridge with such force that it nearly sliced the vessel in half. The *Star of New Zealand* went astern with the result that the 20 foot (6m) wide gapping hole that she had caused rapidly filled with water. The *Pontos* sank 20 minutes later. A voice called out from the *Star of New Zealand*, 'Shall I send you boats', to which Terchan replied 'I am sinking'. The master of the *Star of New Zealand* immediately got off three boats for the stricken crew and passengers, and rescued 12 of them in one of the boats, taking them to Tilbury, where the *Star of New Zealand* was later to receive repairs. However, before arriving at Tilbury the *Star of New Zealand* anchored at Holehaven to discharge part of her cargo of dynamite!

The remaining crew, passengers and livestock of the *Pontos* were adrift in the sea. Many of the animals were already dead and drifting on the surface, while others were trying to swim. One bullock had been completely cut in two by the impact.

The crew and passengers in the two boats not picked up by the *Star of New Zealand* were left to drift in the thick fog, which was not without its own dangers. While drifting they could hear the foghorns of other ships around them. This only served to heighten their anxiety and concern for their safety. Suddenly two large steamships appeared out of the fog, side by side. Had it not been for Terchan's swift response, giving orders to manoeuvre the boats, they would definitely have been swamped or run down. Fortunately, they all survived but were left tossing and bobbing about on the wakes of the two steamers who were completely oblivious to them.

At about 2am, nearly five hours after the collision, a Hastings fishing boat, the *Ellen,* under the command of Benjamin Gallop, could hear people shouting for help and blowing whistles. He pulled up his trawl and tried to find where the voices were coming from. He eventually found one of the drifting boats containing 20 people, including the master, Henrick (second officer), F. Husadel (chief engineer), three cattlemen and three passengers (Miss Eplaie, Miss Hostheide and Mr O.M. Fleischer). It was reported that 'Neither of the ladies were wearing hats'!

These rescued people were taken in the *Ellen* to Hastings where they were looked after by Mr W.H. Gallop, the local agent of the Shipwrecked Mariners Society, in the Shaftesbury Restaurant.

The other boat containing 12 other members of the *Pontos* crew was found by the *Snowdrop* of Aberdeen. They were taken to Dover suffering from exposure.

Good Intent

Date sunk:	21.11.1899
Location:	Goatledge Rock, Warrior Square, St Leonards
Type:	Sailing fishing vessel
Home port:	Hastings
Owner:	Alfred William Bumstead & James Bumstead, Hastings
Master:	Samuel Coussins
No. of crew:	2
Ref:	HS 22.11.1899, 29.11.1899; HN 24.11.1899; HO 25.11.1899

The *Good Intent* was considered to be one of the largest and best of the Hastings fishing fleet at the time. Its master, Samuel Coussins and his two crew, Daniel Martin and Edward Muggeridge, left Hastings beach on the morning of Monday 20th November 1899.

It was at 6.30am the following day that the *Good Intent* was returning to Hastings with its catch. It was low tide, Coussins was at the helm and the other two were busy tending to their catch. When they were off Warrior Square the vessel suddenly struck Goatledge Rock, causing a large hole between the bilge and the keel. The *Good Intent* heeled over and sank within two minutes, which was just long enough for the men to get out of their heavy clothing and sea boots and get into the sea before she went down. Fortunately, as it was low tide, the vessel was proud of the water by 2 or 3 feet (1m), which enabled two of the crew to hang onto the side to await rescue. The third member of the crew hung onto a rope from the vessel. All three were quickly picked up by other local boats and taken back to Hastings.

Later that same morning two local fishing smacks attempted to recover the *Good Intent*, which was only insured by the owners for about half its actual value. The *Good Intent* was slung between two cables from the two smacks but unfortunately the cables snapped due to the excessive strain after moving the vessel about 50 yards (15m) inshore.

A second attempt was made the following evening which was successful, and the *Good Intent* was taken back to Hastings Stade for repairs.

An appeal was launched on behalf of the three men in the following letter to the *Hastings Standard*:

Sir,

Your readers will doubtless have read the account of the sinking of the Hastings fishing boat, Good Intent, *through striking on the rocks near Hastings Pier on Tuesday last. The crew, consisting of three men, Daniel Martin, Mugridge, and Samuel Coussens, the captain, all of whom are married men with families, have lost all their belongings, including clothes and sea boots. The men, although hard working and sober, have been able during the past few months to earn sufficient only to provide for their family needs. As this great misfortune has overtaken them, leaving them for the present without berths, and practically without clothing to go to sea, should berths be provided for them, I beg leave to appeal to the generous public for liberal help for these distressed fishermen – about £16 is needed. Contributions will be gladly received by the owner of the boat Alfred Bumstead, care of Councillor Gallop, Rock-a-Nore-Road, or by*

Yours truly,

H.J. Sanders,

Chaplain Fishermen's Church,
61, Old London Road.

P.S. – The amount collected will be equally divided among the three men.

Sole Bay

Date sunk:	22.11.1899
Location:	7 miles (11km) off Rye harbour
Type:	Sailing fishing dandy
Home port:	Rye
Date built:	1865
Owner:	J. Gallop, Rye
Master:	J.C. Locke
No. of crew:	2
Ref:	SIBI V2 Section 3; HO 25.11.1899; FC 25.11.1899; SEA 3.12.1887; BC 3.12.1887

In December 1897, two years before the collision in which the *Sole Bay* was to become a wreck, a clothes chest was found by the crew floating in Rye Bay. Having opened the chest when they returned to Rye, it was found to contain the property of one Ah Fat Wong, who was the cook on board the 1,200 ton American ship *F.E. Sawyer*. This ship sank at about 6am on Tuesday 22nd November 1887 off Sandgate after colliding with the ocean Steamship Company's steamer *Palinurus*. The *Palinurus* saved all the crew from the *F.E. Sawyer*.

On Wednesday 22nd November 1899 the *Sole Bay,* under J.C. Locke and his two crew, John Ford and Henry Crampton, were trawling about 7 miles (11km) off Rye harbour in clear and fine weather. The men were busying themselves with their work when they were suddenly run down by the steamship *Rockcliff* of West Hartlepool. The *Rockcliff* almost cut the *Sole Bay* in half, and the three men on board had just enough time to get their jolly boat launched before she went down. In the meantime the *Rockcliff* stopped and the three men paddled their jolly boat to her and asked the crew for an oar, which they were given. The *Rockcliff* then carried on its way to Hamburg, because there were a number of local fishing vessels in the area to give the stricken crew assistance. The crew of the *Sole Bay* rowed to the nearest of these which was the Rye trawler, *Forget-Me-Not*, which towed the jolly boat to Hastings and landed the three men safely. Once ashore the men were given rail passes to get back to Rye by Mr W.H. Gallop, the local agent of the Shipwrecked Mariners Society.

SOURCES OF INFORMATION

Books

Bouquet, Michael, *South Eastern Sail*
Hutchinson, Geoff, *Martello Towers: A Brief History*
Larn, Richard and Bridget, *Shipwreck Index of the British Isles – Volume 2* (Lloyd's Register of shipping)
Thomas, R, *Remarkable Shipwrecks* (Andrus & Starr)

Newspapers

Bexhill Chronicle
Cinque Ports Chronicle & E. Sussex Observer
Cinque Ports Chronicle & Southern Advertiser
Eastbourne Chronicle
Eastbourne Gazette
Folkestone Chronicle
Folkestone Express
Folkestone Observer
Hastings & St Leonards Advertiser
Hastings & St Leonards Chronicle
Hastings & St Leonards Gazette
Hastings & St Leonards Independent
Hastings & St Leonards News
Hastings & St Leonards Observer
Hastings & St Leonards Standard
Hastings & St Leonards Times
South Eastern Advertiser
Sussex Agricultural Express
Sussex Express
Sussex Weekly Advertiser

Other

East Sussex County Council Archaeological Department, Lewes, East Sussex

The Brett series of manuscripts held at Hastings Central Library, East Sussex
John Reeley Diary, held at Maidstone County Records Office, Kent
Maritime and Coastguard Agency, Bridlington, Yorkshire
Royal National Lifeboat Institute, Poole, Dorset

ACKNOWLEDGEMENTS

I wish to acknowledge the following for the assistance they have given me in the research and preparation of this book: Roger Bristow and the staff of the reference section, Hastings Central Library; Stuart Norse, service information manager, RNLI, Poole, Dorset; Tony Ellis, deputy district controller, Maritime and Coastguard Agency, Bridlington, Yorkshire; Richard and Bridget Larn for their cooperation in the use of information from their book *Shipwreck Index of the British Isles-Vol. 2*; Steve Cooke for helping with the photographs and my daughter Michelle whose invaluable assistance in the final preparation of this book I could not have done without.

ALPHABETICAL INDEX OF SHIPWRECKS

NAME OF WRECK	DATE	PAGE NO.
Achille	17.7.1883	212
Achille	11.3.1892	263
Active	2.2.1825	43
Adriana	30.11.1802	24
Agnes Campbell	17.11.1871	153
Albion	1827	47
Allison	14.1.1879	178
Amalia	17.12.1816	37
Anna	24.1.1854	98
Anna Maria	6.2.1894	267
Annie	15.8.1890	238
Appollo	18.2.1879	179
Attempt	13.12.1803	25
Belona	1870	143
Benedictoire de Dieu	12.5.1863	124
Betsey	20.2.1831	53
Brothers	13.1.1811	29
Brunswick	2.2.1825	45
Canton	4.12.1859	111
Carnanton	4.12.1859	113
Charles	2.12.1887	229
Charlotte	3.8.1877	162
Chateau Margaux	28.4.1889	235
Clara	29.11.1862	123
Clio	5.7.1876	159
Coastguard galley (unknown)	8.8.1881	198
Coastguard vessel (unnamed)	17.1.1859	106
Collingwood	11.4.1836	63
Commerce	11.12.1810	28

NAME OF WRECK	DATE	PAGE NO.
Commerce	26.9.1878	174
Conrad	23.1.1834	60
Cyrus	15.3.1878	173
Daniel Wheeler	6.3.1862	121
Defence	2.2.1825	44
Diana Grace	11.1.1849	80
Diligence	21.12.1824	41
Donna Maria	25.11.1877	167
Draper	8.10.1857	102
Eagle	1823	39
Ebenezer	10.11.1878	177
Edinburgh	14.3.1879	181
Eliza	22.5.1884	220
Elsa	7.6.1887	228
Elsie Linck	10.11.1876	160
Emma & John	2.6.1860	116
Equator	21.1.1871	147
Esperance	18.9.1891	248
Fairy	2.1.1869	138
Fame	1.2.1831	52
Fancy	8.9.1838	64
Fanny	9.12.1877	169
Franc Picard	27.11.1881	206
Frank	4.7.1897	272
Freak	24.5.1886	227
Friendship	8.8.1881	199
Friends of Liberty	1824	40
George Williams	9.3.1891	242
Georgiana	2.6.1860	115
Good Intent	23.11.1852	89
Good Intent	21.11.1899	227
Guiseppe	23.3.1895	270
Harbinger	2.9.1859	109
Hazard	19.11.1831	54
Henrick von Thorn	15.11.1866	131
Henrietta	9.3.1891	243
Henry	7.7.1848	79
Hermes	5.12.1872	155

NAME OF WRECK	DATE	PAGE NO.
Hopewell	11.12.1810	27
Horten	1.7.1880	184
Hull Packet	26.12.1834	61
Ida Marshall	24.11.1885	225
Innocenza Protetta	14.11.1800	23
Isabella	20.2.1833	56
Isabella	24.9.1883	214
James	27.1.1842	73
James & Emma	2.6.1860	116
Jansson Lina	28.8.1881	205
J.C. Pfluger	11.11.1891	251
John & Ellen	16.11.1882	211
John & James	9.4.1868	137
John & Mary	27.9.1856	100
John Weavel	4.10.1853	97
Juliana	12.12.1887	230
Juno	3.3.1881	196
Kent	30.7.1844	75
Kingston By Sea	1.10.1853	95
La Constance	19.1.1830	51
L'Aimee	21.11.1831	55
Lamburn	18.11.1866	132
Lepanto	6.1.1898	274
Les Trois Amis	26.1.1840	71
Lewes Lass	31.10.1885	223
Linnet	9.3.1891	246
London Packet	07.3.1878	171
Lord Exmouth	18.1.1835	62
Lord Hill	5.12.1849	83
Louisa	26.12.1838	66
Louisa Emilie	27.12.1852	91
Louise	29.6.1861	117
L'Rencon	27.11.1814	32
Margaret	14.2.1813	31
Margaret	14.12.1816	36
Margaret	24.8.1881	204
Mariner	19.3.1893	264
Mary	13.10.1822	38

NAME OF WRECK	DATE	PAGE NO.
Mary Botwood	8.9.1869	142
Mary Anne	31.7.1844	76
Milward	2.2.1825	46
Milward	30.9.1863	126
Minstrel	12.10.1880	189
Nelly	0.11.1810	26
Nelson	29.4.1886	226
Neptune	27.11.1814	33
Nerissa	11.11.1891	257
Nifa	14.9.1893	265
Notre Dame De Mont Carmel	1.1.1855	99
Olaf Trygvasson	17.11.1896	271
Owners Delight	8.6.1851	85
Pearl	14.2.1869	140
Perseverance	27.1.1849	82
Perseverance	17.4.1860	114
Perseverance	30.9.1863	125
Peter Varkevisser	8.8.1897	273
Phoenix	11.1.1849	81
Pilgrim	8.10.1857	104
Pilot Cutter No. 12	16.2.1871	154
Plover	11.3.1889	234
Pontos	31.3.1899	275
Prince	3.3.1881	197
Prince Imperial	8.9.1877	164
Queen Victoria	26.12.1838	70
Regina	15.1.1853	94
Reine Des Patriachs	15.8.1866	130
Robin Hood	21.11.1864	129
Rover	1827	48
Royal Albert	6.6.1870	144
Rushing Water	19.12.1867	136
Rye	20.9.1891	250
Sagitta	18.12.1881	208
Sainte Anne	16.12.1881	207
Sally	12.11.1852	87
Sally & Susannah	6.8.1852	86

NAME OF WRECK	DATE	PAGE NO.
Sarah & Elizabeth	1.10.1888	233
Sceptre	22.12.1824	42
Scruger	5.10.1850	84
Silksworth	23.1.1884	218
Singapore	14.7.1844	74
Sole Bay	22.11.1899	279
Sophia Holten	10.2.1881	194
Speedwell	1.2.1892	262
Startled Fawn	19.12.1867	134
Sudbourne	24.11.1890	241
Sultana	13.6.1885	222
Sussex	26.12.1838	69
Swan	12.12.1884	221
Sweet Hope	20.12.1894	269
Telemachus	10.1.1834	59
Thetis	13.2.1864	127
Thomas Snook	30.6.1862	122
Twee Cornelissen	27.12.1845	77
T.W. Webb	20.5.1871	151
Tyro	3.6.1869	141
Union	4.12.1814	35
Unknown	25.11.1829	50
Unknown stone sloop	11.10.1813	30
Unknown yawl	17.8.1881	202
Velocipede	17.8.1880	185
Vesuvius	7.4.1876	156
Victor Hamille	18.1.1881	193
Victory	3.8.1877	163
Vier Broeders	18.12.1877	170
Volunteer	4.12.1889	236
Warwickshire	29.12.1891	260
Willem Eduard	1.12.1861	119
William	21.1.1827	49
William Pitt	26.12.1838	68
Zeal	4.11.1877	166